How to Become a Clutterologist™

Nancy Miller

A Guide to Becoming a PROFESSIONAL ORGANIZER

CPM
SYSTEMS
PUBLISHING COMPANY
6318 Ridgepath Court
Rancho Palos Verdes, CA 90275-3248
CPMPub@RoundsMiller.com

First Printing, 2009
Second Printing, 2010
Third Printing, 2012
Printed in the United State of America
978-1-891440-68-7

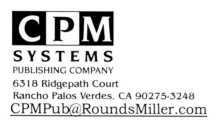

Disclaimer

This book is written with the understanding that the author was not engaged in rendering legal services. The information included has been carefully prepared and is correct to the best of her knowledge as of the publication date. If you require legal or expert advice, the services of professionals should be used. The author disclaims any personal liability, either directly or indirectly, for advice or information presented in this book.

The information as described has been used successfully to obtain profitable business for some of the people who have used it. Although all efforts have been expended to supply the latest in complete, accurate and up-to-date information, it must be understood that the ultimate success of the user is dependent upon market conditions, efforts expended by the user, and other variable factors that are beyond the control of the author, and that neither the users' actual expenses nor profits are guaranteed nor implied.

Throughout this book, trademarked names are used. Rather than put a trademark symbol after every occurrence of the trademarked name, we used the names in an editorial fashion only, and to the benefit of the trademark owner, with no intention of infringement of the trademark.

At the time this edition was printed and released, all of the sites listed were active and accessible to anyone having access to the Internet. Neither the author nor the publisher is responsible for broken links, abandoned sites, or changes that are beyond their control.

You may not incorporate or include Clutterology® and the Clutter Dude™ trademarks in your company name, product name, domain name, or in the name of your service. The name Clutterology® and the Clutter Dude™ graphic are registered trademarks of Nancy Miller, the Clutterologist™. Neither your product name nor the name of your service(s) may be confusingly similar to any Clutterology® and the Clutter Dude™ trademarks. You may not directly or indirectly imply Clutterology® and the Clutter Dude™ sponsorship, affiliation, or endorsement of your product or service.

Reference to Clutterology® and/or the Clutter Dude™ may not be the most prominent visual element on your product or service. Your company name and/or logo, your product or service name, and your graphics should be significantly larger than the reference to the name Clutterology® and/or the Clutter Dude™ trademark.

If your use includes references to a Clutterology® product, the full name of the product must be referenced at the first and most prominent mention (Clutterology® Getting Rid of Clutter and Getting Organized). When referencing any Clutterology® or the Clutter Dude™ trademarks, please mark with a ® or ™ as indicated herein.

You may not shorten or abbreviate any Clutterology® trademarks. Always spell and capitalize the Clutterology® trademarks exactly as they appear herein.

Table of Contents

the ORGANIZING BUSINESS

Section 1: The Organizing Business

So you're thinking about becoming a Professional Organizer? There are currently about 4000 Professional Organizers, dozens of television programs featuring Professional Organizers helping people get organized and thousands of books on how to get organized. Welcome to the ranks.

This manual is for the beginning organizer who wants to build a strong foundation of skills and knowledge in order to launch a successful organizing business.

There are actually three parts to a business. The Organizing Business, Creating the Business (business basics) and Getting the Business (marketing). This manual will not discuss how to organize your clients, because you'll bring that to your business. Another way of saying that is that there is no *right or wrong way* to organize a person. What works for one person doesn't always work for another person. There are a number of books available (new as well as old) that will give you great ideas.

Professional Organizer Job Description - Career as a Professional Organizer

Education and Training: None

Salary: Starting—$25 to $35 per hour

Employment Outlook: Very good

Definition and Nature of the Work
Professional Organizers bring order to everything from office filing systems and medical records to family budgets and bedroom closets. They help businesses and individuals gain more control over time and space, reduce stress, and increase productivity by providing information and ideas, structure, and comprehensive organizational systems.

While some Professional Organizers will organize just about anything for a client, others specialize in a particular area. Those who specialize usually choose an area related to the field in which they worked before becoming organizers. For example, an organizer who previously worked in banking may specialize in organizing financial matters such as bill paying and retirement accounts. Other specialties include residential or office organizing, closet/storage design and organizing, relocation management, records or filing systems management, memorabilia organizing, and time and space management.

Education and Training Requirements
There are no specific educational or training requirements needed to become a Professional Organizer. However, organizers should be experienced and knowledgeable in their area of expertise and be able to provide references for potential clients. Most Professional Organizers enter the field after working for several years in other professions. All organizers must have good communication and management skills and must be detail oriented.

Getting the Job
Prospective organizers can consult the member directory of the National Association of Professional Organizers for names of organization/management consulting firms in their area. Many people who enter the field begin work as free lancers and set up their own small businesses. They advertise in newspapers, magazines, and professional journals to attract clients.

Advancement Possibilities and Employment Outlook
Advancement in this field depends on gaining a reputation for performing quality service. Some Professional Organizers advance by moving from smaller rural markets to more lucrative metropolitan areas. Others start their own businesses after holding positions in large management firms.

The field of professional organizing is growing rapidly, primarily due to the increasing demands placed on people by the complex technology of the Information Age. More and more people are turning to organizers to help them put aspects of their personal and professional lives in order. Therefore, the job outlook for Professional Organizers is very good through the year 2014.

Working Conditions
Professional Organizers generally work out of offices or their own homes. They spend a great deal of time meeting with clients and working at clients' homes and business offices. Many work flexible hours. Professional Organizers also spend time designing organizational plans and negotiating with suppliers.

Earnings and Benefits
Earnings for Professional Organizers vary widely according to qualifications, experience, type of service offered, and geographic area. Organizers may start out with an hourly fee of $25 to $35, while those with more experience may charge as much as $125 per hour. Some organizers charge by the day, collecting as much as $1,500 for an eight-to ten-hour day.

From: http://careers.stateuniversity.com/pages/315/Professional-Organizer.html

How do you become an organizer? Read books, read magazines, visit Web sites, attend a local NAPO chapter meeting, attend a NAPO Conference, and visit Web sites of association organizations like the Institute for Challenging Disorganization (www.ChallengingDisorganization.org) and the National Association of Professional Organizers is NAPO (www.NAPO.net).

If you can't go to a NAPO Conference or don't want to join, you still have access to their information. VW Tapes, PO Box 1058, Manhattan Beach CA 90267 310-726-1004 orders@VWTapes.com www.VWTapes.com. They are the suppliers for the NAPO Conference. It you would like a CD from a conference, they can be ordered directly from here. The local NAPO chapter may have the audios available in their lending library.

Organizing Specialties

There are basically three different marketing areas for a Professional Organizer: residential, small-office home-office (SOHO); and corporations. You may choose to have a different rate for each market. Within these markets, there are numerous specializations. According to NAPO the following is a break-down of organizing specialties:

Residential Organizing Specialties	Business Organizing Specialties
Attention Deficit Disorder	Business coach
Author/writer	Coach for new organizers
Children	Commercial office
Chronically disordered	Electronic management (only)
Closet design and installation	Ergonomics
Closet organizing	Event/meeting planning
Coach for new Professional Organizers	Feng Shui

Electronic management (only)
Estate organizing
Feng Shui
Financial/bookkeeping
Garage/attics/basements
Garage/estate sales
Group training
Kitchens
Languages other than English
Moving/relocation
Office (non-business)
Other rooms
Paper and electronic management
Paper management (only)
People with physical disabilities
Personal coach
Photographs/memorabilia/collections
Product spokesperson
Public speaking
Seniors
Students
Time management

Home office
International travel
Inventory/assets control
Legal offices
Manufacturing
Medical offices
Moving/relocation
National travel
Paper and electronic management
Paper management (only)
Personal coach
Storage/warehouse
Time management

Local Chapters
Joining a local chapter may provide the education and peer support.

Los Angeles Chapter	www.NAPOLA.org	213-486-4477
Sacramento Chapter	www.NAPOsacramento.com	916-765-6104
San Diego Chapter	www.NAPOsandiego.com	619-507-8301
San Francisco Bay Area Chapter	www.NAPO-sfba.org	866-681-2797
Virtual Chapter NAPO-VC	www.NAPO.net	856-380-6828

Code of Ethics
As a Professional Organizer, there is a certain set of expectations by the public. As there are few credentialing requirements for a Professional Organizer, NAPO has a Code of Ethics which outlines many issues and concerns that Professional Organizers face. Here is NAPO's Code of Ethics.

This Code of Ethics is a set of principles to provide guidelines in our professional conduct with our clients, colleagues, and community. As a member of the National Association of Professional Organizers, I pledge to exercise judgment, self-restraint, and conscience in my conduct in order to establish and maintain public confidence in the integrity of NAPO members and to preserve and encourage fair and equitable practices among all who are engaged in the profession of organizing.

Clients Working Relationships
- I will serve my clients with integrity, competence, and objectivity, and will treat them with respect and courtesy.

- I will offer services in those areas in which I am qualified and will accurately represent those qualifications in both verbal and written communications.

- When unable or unqualified to fulfill requests for services, I will make every effort to recommend the services of other qualified organizers and/or other qualified professionals.

- I will advertise my services in an honest manner and will represent the organizing profession accurately.

Confidentiality
- I will keep confidential all client information, both business and personal, including that which may be revealed by other organizers.

- I will use proprietary client information only with the client's permission.

- I will keep client information confidential and not use it to benefit myself or my firm, or reveal this information to others.

Fees
- I will decide independently and communicate to my client in advance my fees and expenses, and will charge fees and expenses which I deem reasonable, legitimate, and commensurate with my experience, the services I deliver, and the responsibility I accept.

- I will make recommendations for products and services with my client's best interests in mind.

Colleagues
- I will seek and maintain an equitable, honorable, and cooperative association with other NAPO members and will treat them with respect and courtesy.

- I will respect the intellectual property rights (materials, titles, and thematic creations) of my colleagues, and other firms and individuals, and will not use proprietary information or methodologies without permission.

- I will act and speak on a high professional level so as not to bring discredit to the organizing profession.

Some other ethical concerns that you may not have considered that may conflict with your personal values are. What if while helping your client organize, you discover:

- a gun
- porn
- illegal drugs
- violations of fire code
- more animals (cats, dogs, etc.) than the city allows

What would you do? How would you handle it?

Although the answers may be easy to think about, when you are working with a client, the answers may be a little gray. Talking to other NAPO members may be a great resource at times like these.

The Institute for Challenging Disorganization is an organization that has documented the level of hoarding by level and degree. This chart has helped me to put into perceptive what a client's environment is.

Clutter-Hoarding Scale

This document is to be used as an assessment/guideline tool only. The Institute for Challenging Disorganization is not responsible for any work performed by a professional organizer or other related professional when using the ICD Clutter – Hoarding Scale

PARAMETERS OF THE SCALE

Five Levels

The ICD has established five levels to indicate the degree of household clutter and/or hoarding from the perspective of a professional organizer or related professional.

The levels in the scale are progressive, with Level I as the lowest and Level V the highest. The ICD considers Level III to be the pivot point between a household that might be assessed as cluttered, and a household assessment that may require the deeper considerations of working in a hoarding environment.

LEVEL	COLOR	LEVEL OF CLUTTER – HOARDING
I	**GREEN**	**LOW**
II	**BLUE**	**GUARDED**
III	**YELLOW**	**ELEVATED**
IV	**ORANGE**	**HIGH**
V	**RED**	**SEVERE**

Five Assessment Categories

Within each level are five specific categories that describe the degree of clutter and/or hoarding potential.

1. Structure and Zoning
Assessment of access to entrances and exits; function of plumbing, electrical, HVAC (any aspect of heating, ventilation or air conditioning) systems and appliances; and structural integrity

2. Animals and Pests
Assessment of animal care and control; compliance with local animal regulations; assessment for evidence of infestations of pests (rodents, insects or other vermin)

3. Household Functions
Assessment of safety, functionality and accessibility of rooms for intended purposes

4. Health and Safety
Assessment of sanitation levels in household; household management of medications for prescribed (Rx) and/or over-the-counter (OTC) drugs

5. Personal Protective Equipment (PPE)
Recommendations for PPE (face masks, gloves, eye shields or clothing that protect wearer from environmental health and safety hazards); additional supplies as appropriate to observational level

THE ICD CLUTTER – HOARDING SCALE > Level I		
LEVEL I	GREEN	LOW
Household environment is considered standard. No special knowledge in working with the chronically disorganized is necessary.		
Structure and Zoning	• All doors, stairways and windows accessible • All plumbing, electrical, HVAC (heating, ventilation and air conditioning) systems fully functional • Installed and functional fire and carbon monoxide (CO) detectors	
Animals and Pests	• Appropriate animal control (behavior and sanitation) • Number of animals in compliance with zoning regulations • No evidence of non-pet rodents or insects	
Household Functions	• No excessive clutter • All rooms being used for intended purposes • All household appliances fully functional • Consistent routine housekeeping and maintenance	
Health and Safety	• Safe and maintained sanitation conditions • No odors (animal, food or natural gas) • Medications: quantity within normal limits; appropriately stored, current dates and child-proof lids as indicated	
Personal Protective Equipment (PPE)	• PPE Optional • First aid kit, hand sanitizer, flashlight and insect repellent	

THE ICD CLUTTER – HOARDING SCALE > Level II		
LEVEL II	BLUE	GUARDED
Household environment requires professional organizers or related professionals who have additional knowledge and understanding of chronic disorganization.		
Structure and Zoning	• One major exit blocked • One major appliance or HVAC device not working for longer than one season (regionally appropriate) • Some plumbing or electrical systems not fully functional • Nonexistent or non-functional fire and carbon monoxide (CO) detectors	
Animals and Pests	• Animals: evidence of inappropriate animal control (behavior and sanitation) • Visible or odorous pet waste • Visible pet fur/hair/feathers • Light to medium evidence of common household pests/insects	
Household Functions	• Clutter obstructs some functions of key living areas • Slight congestion of exits, entrances, hallways and stairs • Some household appliances not fully functional • Inconsistent routine housekeeping and maintenance	
Health and Safety	• Evidence of non-maintained sanitation conditions • Odors related to dirty dishes, food preparation surfaces, laundry, toilets; mildew in bathroom or kitchen • Medications: quantities questionable; expired, current Rx and OTC commingled; haphazard storage; pills not in Rx containers	
Personal Protective Equipment (PPE)	• Light PPE: as needed and suggested • Medical or industrial grade latex or nitrile gloves and heavy-duty leather or cloth work gloves with reinforced palms • Caps (such as baseball) or disposable polyester bouffant caps • Disposable shoe covers • First aid kit, hand sanitizer, flashlight and insect repellent	

<table>
<tr><td colspan="3">THE ICD CLUTTER – HOARDING SCALE > Level III</td></tr>
<tr><td>LEVEL III</td><td>YELLOW</td><td>ELEVATED</td></tr>
<tr><td colspan="3">The ICD considers Level III to be the pivot point between a household environment that can be assessed as cluttered and a household assessment that may require the deeper considerations of working in a hoarding environment. Professional organizers, related professionals or others who are working with Level III household environments should have significant training in chronic disorganization and have developed a helpful community network of resources, especially mental health professionals.</td></tr>
<tr><td>Structure and Zoning</td><td colspan="2">• Outside clutter of items normally stored indoors
• HVAC devices not working for longer than one season (regionally appropriate)
• Nonexistent or non-functional fire and carbon monoxide (CO) detectors
• One part of home exhibits light structural damage (having occurred in preceding six months)</td></tr>
<tr><td>Animals and Pests</td><td colspan="2">• Animal population exceeds local legal regulations
• Evidence of inappropriate animal control
• Inadequate sanitation (fish tank stagnant, reptile aquarium not well maintained, animal odor and waste, bird droppings)
• Audible evidence of pests; medium level of spider webs in house
• Light insect infestation (bed bugs, lice, fleas, cockroaches, ants, silverfish, etc.)</td></tr>
<tr><td>Household Functions</td><td colspan="2">• Clutter obstructing functions of key living areas
• Clutter exists around exits, entrances, hallways and stairs
• At least one room not being used for intended purpose, e.g., items stored in shower; limited bed access or space
• Several appliances not fully functional
• Inappropriate usage of electric appliances and extension cords
• Substandard housekeeping and maintenance
• One or two obvious hazardous materials in small quantities, such as chemical spills, broken glass, etc.</td></tr>
<tr><td>Health and Safety</td><td colspan="2">• Evidence of non-maintained sanitation conditions (food preparation surfaces heavily soiled, dirty dishes, dirty toilets, visible mildew in bathroom or kitchen)
• Odors obvious and irritating
• Garbage cans not in use, full or overflowing
• Presence of accumulated dust, dirt and debris
• Dirty laundry scattered throughout the house
• Medications: Rx and OTC easily accessible to people and pets; presence of expired Rx medications</td></tr>
<tr><td>Personal Protective Equipment (PPE)</td><td colspan="2">• Medium PPE
• Face masks: surgical mask or healthcare particulate respirator mask
• Eye protection and gloves: eyeglasses, safety goggles, medical or industrial grade latex or nitrile gloves; work gloves with reinforced palms
• Disposable coveralls, polyester bouffant caps, work shoes/boots
• First aid kit, hand sanitizer, flashlight and insect repellent</td></tr>
</table>

<table>
<tr><td colspan="3">THE ICD CLUTTER – HOARDING SCALE > Level IV</td></tr>
<tr><td>LEVEL IV</td><td>ORANGE</td><td>HIGH</td></tr>
<tr><td colspan="3">Household environment requires a coordinated collaborative team of service providers in addition to professional organizers and family. Such providers might include mental health professionals, social workers, financial counselors, pest and animal control officers, crime scene cleaners, licensed contractors and handypersons. Mental health and/or medical and financial issues are frequently involved.</td></tr>
<tr><td>Structure and Zoning</td><td colspan="2">• Excessive outdoor clutter of items normally stored indoors
• HVAC devices not working for longer than one year
• Nonexistent or non-functional fire and carbon monoxide (CO) detectors
• Structural damage to home existing longer than six months
• Water damaged floors, damaged walls and foundations, broken windows, doors or plumbing
• Odor or evidence of sewer backup</td></tr>
<tr><td>Animals and Pests</td><td colspan="2">• Animal population exceeds local ordinances
• Evidence of poor animal sanitation; destructive behavior
• Excessive spiders and webs
• Bats, squirrels, rodents in attic or basement (audible and visible)
• Medium insect infestation (bedbugs, lice, fleas, cockroaches, ants, silverfish, etc.)</td></tr>
<tr><td>Household Functions</td><td colspan="2">• Diminished use of and accessibility to key living areas
• Several rooms cluttered to extent they cannot be used for intended purposes, e.g., items stored in shower; limited bed access or space
• Clutter inhibits access to exits, entrances, hallways and stairs
• Inappropriate storage of hazardous/combustible materials, e.g., gasoline, leaking paint or chemicals
• Appliances used inappropriately, e.g., refrigerator being used for storing non-food items
• Improper use of electric space heaters, fans or extension cords</td></tr>
<tr><td>Health and Safety</td><td colspan="2">• Rotting food, organic contamination
• Expired, leaking or buckling cans and/or jars
• Dishes and utensils unusable
• No linens on beds; sleeping on mattress, chair or floor; infestation of bedding and/or furniture
• Mold and/or mildew obvious; visible moisture or standing water
• Medications: Rx and OTC easily accessible to people and pets; presence of expired Rx medications</td></tr>
<tr><td>Personal Protective Equipment (PPE)</td><td colspan="2">• Full PPE
• Face masks: surgical mask, healthcare particulate respirator mask, or respirator with organic filter(s)
• Safety goggles; medical or industrial grade latex or nitrile gloves; heavy duty work gloves
• Disposable coveralls, caps, and shoe covers; work shoes/boots
• First aid kit, hand sanitizer, headlamp/flashlight and insect repellent</td></tr>
</table>

<table>
<tr><td colspan="3">THE ICD CLUTTER – HOARDING SCALE > Level V</td></tr>
<tr><td>LEVEL V</td><td>RED</td><td>SEVERE</td></tr>
<tr><td colspan="3">Household environment will require intervention from a wide range of professionals. Professional organizers should not work alone in a Level V environment. A collaborative team of related professionals needs to be assembled to create and implement clearly defined goals and negotiated timetables. Members might include family, mental health professionals, social workers, building manager, zoning, fire, and/or safety agents. The individual with a Level V home might be involved in legal proceedings, such as a conservatorship, guardianship, divorce, custody, eviction or condemnation proceedings. Formal written agreements among the parties should be in place before proceeding.</td></tr>
<tr><td>Structure and Zoning</td><td colspan="2">• Extreme indoor/outdoor clutter; foliage overgrowth; abandoned machinery
• Inadequate or nonexistent ventilation; HVAC systems not working
• Non-existent or non-functional fire and carbon monoxide (CO) detectors
• Water damaged floors, walls and foundation; broken windows, doors or plumbing
• Unreliable electrical, water, and/or sewer septic systems; odor or evidence of sewer backup
• Irreparable damage to exterior and interior structure
• Nonexistent or non-functional fire and carbon monoxide (CO) detectors</td></tr>
<tr><td>Animals and Pests</td><td colspan="2">• Animals at risk and dangerous to people due to behavior, health and numbers
• Pervasive spiders, mice, rats, squirrels, raccoons, bats, snakes, etc.
• Heavy insect infestation (bed bugs, lice, fleas, cockroaches, ants, silverfish, etc.)</td></tr>
<tr><td>Household Functions</td><td colspan="2">• Key living spaces not usable
• All rooms not used for intended purposes
• Exits, entrances, hallways and stairs blocked
• Toilets, sinks and tubs not functioning
• Hazardous conditions obscured by clutter
• Appliances unusable
• Hazardous and primitive use of kerosene, lanterns, candles, fireplace/woodstove as primary source of heat and/or light</td></tr>
<tr><td>Health and Safety</td><td colspan="2">• Human urine and excrement present
• Rotting food; organic contamination; expired, leaking or buckled cans and/or jars
• Dishes and utensils buried or nonexistent
• Beds inaccessible or unusable due to clutter or infestation
• Pervasive mold and/or mildew; moisture or standing water
• Medications: Rx and OTC easily accessible to people and pets; presence of expired Rx medications</td></tr>
</table>

Personal Protective Equipment (PPE)	• Full PPE required • Face masks: healthcare particulate respirator mask or respirator with organic filter(s) • Safety goggles; medical or industrial grade latex or nitrile gloves; heavy duty gloves • Disposable coveralls, caps and shoe covers; work shoes/boots • First aid kit, hand sanitizer, headlamp/flashlight and insect repellent

ICD gratefully acknowledges the writers of the 2011 revised edition: Kristin Bergfeld, Sheila Delson, CPO-CD®, Randi B. Lyman, CPO-CD®, Lynn Mino, CPO-CD® and Heidi Schulz, CPO-CD®; and the original writers, Sheila Delson, Cindy Glovinsky, Terry Prince and Heidi Schulz.

Certified Professional Organizer

Certification is a **voluntary**, **industry-led** effort that benefits the members of the organizing profession, as well as the public. It is a recognition of professionals who have met specific minimum standards, and proven through examination and client interaction that they possess the body of knowledge and experience required for certification. This program recognizes and raises industry standards, practices and ethics. For the public, while the CPO designation is not an endorsement or recommendation, certification of Professional Organizers maximizes the value received from the products and services provided by a CPO.

To be eligible to sit for the CPO examination, a candidate must meet the following eligibility requirements. BCPO is required to audit a certain percentage of all applications. In the event of an audit, the candidate must be prepared to provide supporting documentation for these requirements.

Qualified candidates must have a minimum of a high school diploma or equivalent.

As a part of the application process, candidates must agree to adhere to the Code of Ethics for Certified Professional Organizers.

Candidates must be prepared to document a total of 1,500 hours of paid work experience in the last three (3) years. This paid work experience may include but is not limited to on-site organizing, coaching, consulting, training, virtual organizing, interactive workshops and speaking engagements, which, through client collaboration, transfers, teaches or demonstrates organizing skills.

Up to 250 substitute hours of the required 1,500 can be earned via college degrees, continuing education courses or professional development activities in the organizing field. Substitute hours may also be earned via organizing related writing and speaking engagements, or relevant paid work experience prior to becoming an organizer and accrued in the three years prior to the application date, as detailed below.

Candidates may claim a maximum of 250 hours of credit towards the required 1,500 hours of paid work experience from one or more of the following substitute categories:

Formal Education (non-cumulative, 100 hours credit maximum): AA Degree, 50 hours credit, Bachelor's Degree, 75 hours credit, Advanced Degree, 100 hours credit.

Organizing-Related Professional Activities: (within the last 3 years), Paid speaking engagements, actual hours, maximum of 10 hours credit, Mentor/Mentee/Apprenticeship, actual hours, maximum of 10 hours credit, Publishing books, 20 per book, maximum of 40 hours credit, Authoring articles (minimum 500 words per article), 10 per published article, maximum of 30 hours credit, Professional Association Membership, maximum of 10 hours credit, Trainer/Teacher, maximum of 10 hours credit, Serving on an Organizing Entity's Board of Directors, maximum of 10 hours credit, Volunteer Work as an Organizer, maximum of 10 hours credit.

Continuing Education Courses relating to Organizing (within the last 3 years): For each course, the candidate may claim the actual hours attended, to a cumulative total of 250 hours. Sixty minutes of coursework is equal to one credit hour regardless of any number of continuing education credits (CEUs) another institution may have awarded for completion of the course.

Relevant Paid Work Experience Prior to Becoming an Organizer: 25 hours credit per full-time year (maximum 3 years or 75 hours credit.) Experience must include the same criteria for teaching, transfer, or demonstration of organizing skills as described in the 1500 hours requirement.

Military Service: 10 hours credit per year (maximum of 5 years or 50 hours credit) for military service.

Recertification: After initial certification, recertification is required every three (3) years. To recertify, a CPO must assert to continuing practice as a Professional Organizer, pay the Annual Maintenance Fees, and either (a) earn 45 eligible continuing education units during the 3-year recertification period or (b) retake and pass the CPO examination.

If a CPO chooses to recertify by examination and fails, certification is immediately revoked. Provided the candidate meets the current eligibility requirements for initial certification, he or she would be eligible to submit a new application to take the current examination as a new candidate future examinations.

The annual maintenance fee is currently $70 per year. Each CPO will automatically receive an invoice prior to his or her anniversary date each year.

Examination Content

The CPO examination is based upon a properly conducted Job Task Analysis, which empirically defines the necessary competencies for the successful practice of organizing. The major domains on the examination are:

Foundations of Professional Organizing 25 percent
Legal and Ethical Considerations 5 percent
Preliminary Assessment 20 percent
Action Plan Development 20 percent
Action Plan Implementation and Project Management 20 percent
Evaluation, Follow-up, and Maintenance 10 percent

Institute for Challenging Disorganization (ICD) provides five levels of certificates and certification.

Level I Specialty Certificates
Foundation Certificate in Chronic Disorganization
Certificate of Study in Basic ADD Issues with the CD Client
Certificate of Study in Client Administration
Certificate of Study in Basic Physical Conditions Affecting the CD Client
Certificate of Study in Understanding the Needs of the Elderly CD Client
Certificate of Study in Learning Styles and Modalities
Certificate of Study in Basic Mental Health Conditions and Challenges Affecting the CD Client
Certificate of Study in Basic Hoarding Issues with the CD Client
Certificate of Study in Understanding the Needs of the Student CD Client
Certificate of Study in Life Transitions

Level II Specialist Certificates
CD Specialist
ADD Specialist
Hoarding Specialist

Level III Certified Professional Organizer in Chronic Disorganization
CPO-CD Overview

Level IV ICD Training Program Mentor
Level IV Mentoring Program Overview
Level V ICD Master Trainer in CD and Organization
Level IV Mentoring Program Overview

Resources

As an organizer, you probably are always on the lookout for resources. Both for yourself and your clients. Here are some resources for you to check out.

Professional Organizing Manuals

There are several Professional Organizers that have written manuals on becoming a Professional Organizer. Most can be purchased at www.OnlineOrganizing.com. I have not purchased any of these manuals.

1. A Manual for Professional Organizers Cyndi Seidler 143-pages $25.00

2. Client Relationship Management Debra Milne 109-pages $49.95

3. Create Your Business as an Organizer Debra Milne 144-pages $49.95

4. Everything You Need to Know about a Career as a Professional Organizer Sara Pedersen 79-pages $55.00

5. Marketing Basics for Organizers Debra Milne 112-pages $49.95

6. Secrets of a Professional Organizer Janet Hall 170-pages $49.95

7. The Professional Organizer's Complete Business Guide Lisa Steinbacher 133-pages $19.95

Books to Help Clients

1. Clutterology® Getting Rid of Clutter and Getting Organized Nancy Miller

2. Confessions of an Organized Homemaker 1558703616 Deniece Schofield

3. How to Be Organized in Spite of Yourself 0451164695 Sunny Schlenger

4. Making Time Work for You A Guide to Productive Time Management 0968367003 Harold Taylor. I love Harold Taylor's style. He is practical and down to earth. Very good at time management.

5. Records Management 081440295X Susan Z. Diamond. This book is very good and goes into details on how to file. For me, it's hard to read because of all the detail.

6. Sidetracked Home Executives™ 978-0446677677 Pam Young, Peggy Jones. I like this book as it breaks down all a person's tasks into daily, weekly, monthly, etc. task and an easy way to maintain this system. This is an older book and may be easier to find at a library.

7. Working Smart How to Accomplish More in Half the Time 0446353566 Michael LeBoeuf Ph.D.

8. Not Buying It Judith Levine 978-0743269360. This journalist decides not to purchase anything other than food for a year. Insight into all the things we think we have to have.

Don Aslett - I love the style of Don Aslett! For me, reading his simple and short books take a long time because my mind starts to brainstorm. So many good ideas.

- Clutter's Last Stand 978-1593373290
- Done! How to Accomplish Twice As Much in Half the Time 978-1593375072
- For Packrats Only 978-0937750254
- How to Handle 1,000 Things at Once 978-0937750193
- Is There Life After Housework? 978-1593375065
- The Office Clutter Cure 978-1593373320
- Weekend Makeover 978-1593374860

Emilie Barnes - Emilie Barnes is an OK author on getting organized. However, she is a Christian author which may appeal to you or your clients.

- 101 Ways to Clean Out the Clutter 978-0736922630
- 500 Time-Saving Hints for Every Woman 978-0736918466
- Cleaning up the Clutter 978-0736909792
- Emilie's Creative Home Organizer 978-0736914451
- More Hours in My Day 978-0736922531
- Simple Secrets to a Beautiful Home 978-0736909693

Stephanie Culp – One of the first people to write about organizing and one of the first members of NAPO. Her books can be considered *the basics* which means they stand the test of time, and are as good today as when they were first written.

- Conquering the Paper Pile-Up 978-0898794106
- How to Conquer Clutter 978-0898793628
- Organized Closets and Storage 978-0898793901
- Stephanie Culp's 12-Month Organizer and Project Planner 978-1558703605
- Streamlining Your Life 978-0898794625

Barbara Hemphill - Barbara has the trademark Taming the Paper Tiger™. She began with a book and now has a software program that you can become a consultant with and train/sell to clients.

- Love It or Lose It 978-1884798276
- Simplify Your Workday 978-0762100989
- Taming the Office Tiger 978-0812927122
- Taming the Paper Tiger at Home 978-0938721970
- Taming the Paper Tiger at Work 978-0938721581
- Taming the Paper Tiger 978-0938721192

Julie Morgenstern - Julie use to be the favorite of the media and Oprah. Although I didn't think her books were that good, some people love her style.

- Making Work Work 978-1413290257
- Never Check E-Mail In the Morning 978-0743250887
- Organizing from the Inside Out for Teenagers 978-0805064704
- Organizing from the Inside Out 978-0805075892
- SHED Your Stuff, Change Your Life 978-0743250900
- Time Management from the Inside Out 978-0805075908

Peter Walsh - The current favorite of the media for organizing. Peter started out as a teacher and became the star of Clean Sweeps. He is the current darling of Oprah Winfrey. He is practical and has great ideas.

- Does This Clutter Make My Butt Look Fat? 978-1416560173
- Enough Already! 978-1416560197
- How to Organize (Just About) Everything 978-0743254946
- It's All Too Much 978-1439149560

Stephanie Winston - Along with Stephanie Culp, Stephanie Winston was one of the first authors to break out as an organizer. You could say that the profession of Professional Organizers started here. Although the books have been updated, sometimes I still find the information out-dated, but they are classics.

- Getting Organized 978-0446694131
- The Organized Executive 0446676969
- Stephanie Winston's Best Organizing Tips 978-0684818245
- Organized for Success 978-1400047598

Professional Organizers - Although being a member of NAPO/ICD doesn't make you a good author, the following book are by professional organizers.

1. ADD-Friendly Ways to Organize Your Life Judith Kolberg 978-1583913581 (NAPO)

2. How to Be Organized in Spite of Yourself Sunny Schlenger 978-0451197467
3. Making Peace with the Things in Your Life Cindy Glovinsky 978-0312284886 (NSGCD)
4. One Thing At a Time Cindy Glovinsky 978-0312324865 (NSGCD)
5. Organize Your Office In No Time Monica Ricci 978-0789732187 (NAPO)
6. Organizing for the Creative Person Dorothy Lehmkuhl 978-0517881644
7. Organizing Magic Sandra Felton 0800730992 (NAPO)
8. Organizing Plain and Simple Donna Smallin 978-1580174480 (NAPO)
9. Simplify Your Space Marcia Ramsland 0849915112 (NAPO)
10. The Beverly Hills Organizer's Home Organizing Bible Linda Koopersmith 978-1592331543 (use to teach at the Learning Annex)
11. The Organized Life Stephanie Denton 978-1581808636 (NAPO)
12. The Organized Student Donna Goldberg 978-0743270205 (NAPO)

Other Authors

- File...Don't Pile Pat Dorff 978-0312289317
- Getting Things Done David Allen 978-0142000281
- Good Things for Organizing Martha Stewart 978-0609805947
- Leave the Office Earlier Laura Stack 978-0767916264
- Organized to Be the Best! Susan Silver 0944708366
- Organizing from the Right Side of the Brain Lee Silber 978-0312318161
- The Time Trap Alec Mackenzie 978-0814413388

Catalogs, Stores and Web Sites

There are so many additional resources to help people get organized. You will have your favorites, however, here are a few for you to check out and see if they will be helpful to you or your clients.

1-800-Got Junk
North America's largest junk removal service. They do all the loading into their truck, and then your junk is recycled, taken to a transfer station, or sent to a landfill. Pricing is based on your city, volume of material, and the nature of the material. They'll take construction materials, garden refuse, furniture appliances, and other items. No hazardous waste accepted. www.1800GotJunk.com.

Century Photo Products and Accessories
PO Box 2393
Brea CA 92822
800-767-0777
www.CenturyPhoto.com
This company has products that are archival safe.

The Clever Container Co.
23411 Jefferson Ste 110
Clair Shores MI 48080
www.clevercontainer.com
www.organizingjustgotfun.com
Do you remember the old Tupperware parties. This is a company that has consultants that sells organizing products through parties showing people how to use the products. About $240 to get started into the program as an independent consultant.

ClosetMaid
www.ClosetMaid.com

Closets by Design
800-293-3744
www.ClosetsByDesign.com
Both of these stores have innovative systems for build-in systems for closets and other spaces.

The Container Store
800-786-7315
www.ContainerStore.com
Lots of goodies for organizers

www.CraigsList.com
A great place to get rid of or sell clients items. An alternative to eBay.com. You might want to check out **www.FreeCycle.com** which is a giveaway sight.

Creative Memories
2815 Clearwater Rd
St. Cloud MN 56302-1839
800-468-9335
Use creative scrapbook albums to preserve photos, stories and memorabilia.

Debt-Proof Newsletter (Mary Hunt)
PO Box 2135
Paramount CA 90723-8135
562-630-6472
www.CheapSkateMonthly.com
Newsletter $29
This newsletters has tons of ideas on how to reduce consumerism. There is a section of the newsletter called Tiptionary where people write their tips. Also review new books and suggests Web sites to help people. She also has **books** (Debt-Proof Living 978-0976079118) that may be of interest.

Exposures
2800 Hoover Road
Stevens Point WI 54481
800-222-4947
www.ExposuresOnline.com
This company has products that are archival safe.

EZ Pocket
$27.95 plus $4.95 shipping and handling.
PO Box 2328
Basalt CO 81621
ezpocket@compuseve.com
$27.95 plus $4.95 shipping and handling.
EZ Pocket is a monthly calendar that hangs on the back of a door (or on the wall). Also available is a week at a glance which with a pocket for Monday, Tuesday, Wednesday,

Thursday, Friday with pockets large enough to store legal size folders. This system can be adapted for use for projects (Girls Scouts, church, budget, etc.).

Frontgate
9180 Le Saint Drive
Fairfield OH 45014
800-626-6488
www.Frontgate.com
This is a more upscale catalog. There are a lot of gadgets that can be used for organizing. Great to look at and get ideas.

Hold Everything
800-421-2264
www.Williams-SonomaInc.com
This is a more upscale catalog. There are a lot of gadgets that can be used for organizing. Great to look at and get ideas.

Home Trends
1450 Lyell Avenue
Rochester NY 14606-9930
www.HomeTrendsCatalog.com
They have a lot of inexpensive and mid range gadgets that help to get people organized.

Improvements
800-642-2112
www.ImprovementsCatalog.com
This is a more upscale catalog. There are a lot of gadgets that can be used for organizing. Great to look at and get ideas.

The Kitchen Collection
Maria Baker
9 Narvaez Way
Hot Springs Village AR 71909
The Recipe Index $12.95
Recipes from Our Family Tree $13.95
For cookbook collectors, the book is designed to help you find the recipe you want when you want it.

Lakeshore Learning
www.LakeshoreLearning.com
This is a web site for teachers. Every once and while, you will find a great idea (or two). Their prices tend to be a little pricey.

Levenger
420 South Congress Avenue
Delray Beach FL 33445-4696
800-544-0880
www.Levenger.com
Tools for the serious reader! This is neat for note cards, books and the desk. Tends to be a little pricey.

Lillian Vernon Corporation
Virginia Beach, VA 23479
800-285-5555
www.LillianVernon.com

Marukai 99 Super Store
If you have any Japanese super stores in your neighborhood, do check them out. They have all kinds of neat containers and things for organizing. Take the product with you that you want the containerize because the sizes are slightly different than American sizes. Some of the products don't last forever.

Mobile Office Outfitter
800-426-3453
www.MobileGear.com
If your office is your car, here are some great solutions.

Mr. Handyman
877-674-2639
www.MrHandyman.com
Mr. Handyman is a franchise to help with almost everything. They are licensed in many different area (like electrical) and have their own tools. They charge by the half hour and accomplish tasks quickly.

Neatnix Organizers
3979 Lockridge St
San Diego CA 92102
619-266-2662 or 800-683-6328
Neatnix has a variety of practical, useable organizing products. Their most popular are: wire basket or drawer organizers (no tools needed and fits all sizes), jewelry stax, and sox box.

www.OnlineOrganizing.com
In addition to being a great place to find almost everything for organizing, they send out two newsletters a month. One on getting organized and another on being a better business person.

DOING THE SPRING FLING

www.Organize.com
Riverside CA 92504-1107
800-600-9817
www.Organize.com
If I purchased a lot of stuff, it would be here. They have some great and unusual gadgets and the prices are mid-range.

www.OrganizedGreetings.com
Donna Smallin Kuper CEO
9302 E Princess Dr
Mesa AZ 85207
480-634-4086
They have a line of cards (thank you, referral, etc.) for Professional Organizers.

Real Simple Magazine
Time Customer Service
Attention: Consumer Affairs
3000 University Center Drive
Tampa, Florida 33612-6408
www.RealSimple.com
$26/year

Spoon Sisters
www.SpoonSisters.com
This site is hard to explain. They don't have a lot of stuff. What they have is useful and unique. Check it out.

Sporty's Preferred Living
2001 Sporty's Dr
Batavia OH 45103
www.Sportys.com
Although Sporty's is a little more for sports things, it has great ideas for containing sport stuff.

Stacks & Stacks
1045 Hensley Street
Richmond, CA 94801
800-761-5222
www.StacksAndStacks.com
If I purchased a lot of stuff, it would be here. They have some great and unusual gadgets and the prices are mid-range.

Taylor Gifts
600 Cedar Hollow Road
PO Box 1776
Paoli PA 19301-0921
800-803-9400
www.TaylorGifts.com

Television Programs

There are a number of programs on television to help people get organized. These programs are edited for television and there is more going on before and after filming. In other words, don't expect to get your client's whole house organized in two days.

Managing Client's Expectations: remind the client that these shows are made for entertainment and are edited. For instance, Clean Sweep may be filmed in two days, but they have pre-planned everything when the camera arrives (layout, supplies, designs, budget). Although there may be an organizer and a designer, there are 10 to 15 people also helping out. Hours spent on those two days are 270 or more hours!

Antiques Roadshow on PBS show people bring in family stuff and coming out with items worth millions. A great show for getting an education on what may or may not have value, what makes it valuable, etc.

Most items brought into the Roadshow are truly stuff—not worth much. There are hundreds of people passing through the doors and hoping that their stuff is worth something. In addition, each person passing through the door is charged a small fee.

Clean House on the Style Network. The premise of this show is to sell enough things from the house at a yard sale to use in the design of the house. If enough money is not made at the yard sale, then the design falls short. The previous host was Niecy Nash and now it is Tempestt Bledsoe. The focus is more on the yard sale and designing. Mark Brunetz, the designer could be called the star of the show. You will not learn much about how to organize. This is only filmed in the Los Angeles area. The nationwide program is Clean House: Search for the Messiest Home in the Country. 1-hour in length.

Clean House: New York on the Style Network. This show is different than the LA based program. They find items in the family home to sell to dealers (antiques, coins, sports, etc), then there is a live auction followed by an indoor yard sale. A good show for creative storage solutions as New York typically has small properties and people need every inch they can find or design for additional space. 1-hour in length.

Clean Sweep on The Learning Channel (TLC). Two days, two rooms, a Professional Organizer and a professional interior designer. They remove all the stuff from the two rooms and take it to the yard. The second day begins with a yard sale and then the reveal. 1-hour in length.

Confessions: Animal Hoarding on Animal Plant. This is new to me and I am just becoming aware of the situation and show. 1-hour in length. I didn't think I could watch this but it is very well done. It is about the animals and finding good homes for them. Not the shock and horror that *Hoarders* sometimes creates.

Extreme Clutter on OWN (Oprah Winfrey Network). Peter helps people with two rooms over two days. What's slightly different about this program is that *a friend* comes in the second day to assist as Peter leaves the family to work on their own. I believe that Peter often crosses the line of Professional Organizer to therapist. 1-hour in length. The first season this was called Enough Already! With Peter Walsh

Hannah Help Me! on PBS. Here is a snipet from her Web site. "Hi! I'm Hannah Keeley. You may have seen me hosting my television series, "Hannah, Help Me!"—the show where I visit an overwhelmed mom and help her get her life back on track. It seems like I have my act together, right? Well, mama, let me tell you something. It wasn't always like that. Trust me."

Hoarders on A&E. This is one of the newer shows on TV (2009/2012). They have two people that are hoarders who work with a therapist and Professional Organizer. At the end of a specific time, the home is cleaned up. This program gives you an awareness of the level of how much stuff many people have. As this program also works with a therapist, there is some insight with how the professionals work with hoarders. 1-hour in length.

Hoarding: Buried Alive on TLC. This is a newer show and seems to take on a realistic view of what is wrong (entertaining) about all the other television programs on getting organized. The process of working with the client and the slow process of going through their stuff and the detailed story of each item is very realistic. 1-hour in length.

How Clean Is Your House? on the Lifetime Channel. Kim and Aggie have crossed the pond to tidy up America one filthy house at a time. Great show for tips and tricks for cleaning dirt. This show is more cleaning than organizing. The program follows-up with the person two weeks afterwards to see if they have gone back to their old ways. ½-hour in length.

For me this show is difficult to take. They show how dirty and filthy the house is. The gals are funny and have personality. One loves to stick her nose into everything and smell it. They also take samples of areas, sending the results to a lab and sharing with the client what types of creepy things were lurking in their home.

The Life Laundry on BBCAmerica hosted by Dawna Walters. This program organizes several rooms per episode. It is based in Britain. It is fun to see the ancestral clutter and the car boot sales (similar to a swap meet). ½-hour in length.

Although the American version became Clean Sweep, this was a wonderful show for insight into a different world. In England, houses are smaller, there is little closet space, little yards and true antiques. Frequently the cleaning out of the room to the front yard was to a neighboring school soccer field or indoor gym. Instead of having a yard sale, the items were sold at a boot sale. More like an American swap meet, where the items were sold out of the back of the car's trunk (boot). Any items not sold then were deposited into a crusher by the home owner.

Mission: Organization on the Home and Garden TV channel (HGTV). They condense many hours to fit the ½-hour format creating the illusion that it only takes two days to do.

The two things I can guarantee you about this show is that they are going to paint the walls (and maybe do something with the floor) and spend lots of money. A NAPO-LA member was on one of the first episodes. What you didn't see was the drive way. All the stuff was just left on the driveway. The show didn't let the organizer help the client.

Neat hosted on the Fit (and also on Discover) by Hellen Buttigieg in Toronto airs on various channels (check your local listing). ½-hour in length. Hellen deals with some difficult organizational problems such as one client who didn't want anyone to touch her stuff.

The Amandas on Style Network. I won't call this a behind the scenes with an organizing business, but Amanda is a professional organizer and she has several assistants. They have very high end jobs and shows up wearing high heels. It's entertaining. 1-hour in length.

Trading Spaces on The Learning Channel (TLC). Two sets of neighbors exchange houses and spend the weekend painting and decorating the other's home in a weekend. Although this is a design show, many people watch it for organizing ideas. One of the trademarks of the show is that at the end of the first night, the couples are given homework.

What The Sell?! On the Learning Channel (TLC) (2011). Three ladies in the Chicago area have a pawn shop or antique shop. It is very romantic because everyone that comes in has great stuff and get a very good price for their items (a couple hundred). One gal had Queen Victoria's nylons that were worth thousands. Your client's expectations might be similar to what they see on the *Antique Roadshow* is that everything and anything is worth more than they expect and the effort is so minimal, why are you suggesting that they get rid of it instead of selling it?

Miscellaneous Television Shows
There has been some single episode, or short run series that didn't make it for very long that you may want to keep an eye out for (or not):

Help! I'm a Hoarder 1-hour (2007). The program followed a two hoarders in different parts of the United States and interviewed medical professionals. Not very entertaining but informative.

I'm Pregnant and ... "a hoarder" 30 minutes (2010).

Ultimate Cleaners: "for health and home" 30 minutes (2011) TLC. A family of extreme cleaners. This series (if it is a series, I haven't been able to find it) looks like it could be interesting to watch and learn from.

Associations For You To Join or Know About

Keep these organizations names close at hand. Clients may need them. The ability to provide additional resources and contacts for your clients is a part of your hidden talents!

American Society of Appraisers
800-272-8258
http://appraisers.org

Appraisers Association of America
212-889-5404

ARMA International (American Record Management Association)
4200 Somerset, Suite 215
Prairie Village, KS 66208-5287
913-341-3808
www.ARMA.org
This organization is about record management both paper and electronic. They have tons of information.

Association of Image Consultants International (AICI)
www.AICI.org
515-282-5500

Attention Deficit Disorder Association
www.ADD.org

International Society of Appraisers
230 E Ohio St. Ste 400
Chicago, IL 60611
isa@isa-appraisers.org

888-472-4732 or 312-224-2567
www.isa-appraisers.org

National Association of Professional Organizers (NAPO)
15000 Commerce Parkway Suite C
Mount Laurel, NJ 08054
856-380-6828
NAPO@NAPO.net
www.NAPO.net
Membership fee from $200-$230 per year depending on the level. Your first year you will probably be a provisional. Then joining the local chapter ($125 dues) and meeting costs.

National Association of Senior Move Managers (NASMM)
877-606-2766
www.NASMM.org

National Concierge Assn
www.nationalconciergeassociation.com

Int'l Concierge & Lifestyle Management Assn
www.ICLMA.org

Institute for Challenging Disorganization
formerly the National Study Group of Chronic Disorganization (NSGCD)
1693 S Hanley Rd
St. Louis MO 63144
314-416-2236
www.ChallengingDisorganization.org
Their mission is to benefit people affected by chronic disorganization. The ICD explores, develops and communicates information, organizing techniques and solutions to Professional Organizers, related professionals and the public.
Membership fee run about $250 per year. There are no local chapters.

Real Estate Staging Association (REASA)
888-201-8687
www.RealEstateStagingAssociation.com

Sotheby's Appraisal Department
212-606-7000
www.Sothebys.com

Associations for Your Client

Clutter Anonymous
PO Box 91413
Los Angeles CA 90009-1413
Contact a local 12-step program in your area for additional information.

Debtors Anonymous
General Service Office
PO Box 920888
Needham MA 02492-0009
800-421-2383 or 781-453-2743
office@debtorsanonymous.org

www.DebtorsAnonymous.org

Fly Lady (Marla Cilley)
FlyLady@flylady.net
www.FlyLady.net
Sends multiple daily e-mail message to motivate to un-clutter now. This is great if you are a stay-at-home individual and on your computer. She will send you a couple of e-mails daily. The premise is that you are to stop what you're doing and go and do what she tells you. The activity is a maximum of fifteen minutes. Some core concepts of the Fly Lady is that you should always make your bed. The bed is a large portion of the bedroom and by doing this, you accomplish a lot. You sink should be free of dishes (dirty or drying) and be sparkling. She has a book Sink Reflections 978-0553382174.

Messies Anonymous
5025 SW 114th Avenue
Miami FL 33165
305-271-8404
www.Messies.com
To receive a sample of the newsletter, send a self-addressed stamped envelope.

Charities

Here is a list of charities that has been complied with assistance from students that have taken our seminars. The criteria was items that a person has around the house that are looking for a *good home*. There are two way to use this information. The first is a cause. If you or your client wants to support the animal rescue, the contact information is listed.

If you or your client are looking to donate folding chairs, look at the second half of the chart. There look at the item and then find who is interested in those specific items.

1736 Family Crisis Center Shelter Partnership
21707 Hawthorne Blvd Ste 300
Torrance CA 90503
310-543-9900
www.1736familycrisiscenter.org
Clothes, household items and toys.

Animal Rescue
Animal Shelter
Humane Society
various locations
Search Google for Web sites and specific information
Blankets, cleaning supplies, towels, sheets, and t-shirts.

ASBA (The Arizona Small Business Association)
4130 E Van Buren Ste 150
Phoenix AZ 85008-6947
602-265-4563
www.asba.com
Appliances, computers, TV's, small electronics, anything with a cord.

Asset Network for Education Worldwide (ANEW)
CA
213-943-4400
Carpet, ceiling fans, doors, hardware and all furniture.

Blossom Birth
299 S California Ave
Palo Alto CA 94306
650-321-2326
Baby care items, books (pregnancy, birth, babies, and parenting) in other languages, baby clothes, DVDs, and maternity clothes.

Books for the Barrios
1121 Wiget Lane
Walnut Creek, CA 94598
510-687-7701
National Geographic magazines.

Books for Treats
San Jose CA
408-998-7977
www.BooksForTreats.org
info@booksfortreats.org
Children's books.

Bridge to Asia Foreign Trade Services
Pier 23
San Francisco CA 94111
415-678-2990
www.bridge.org asianet@bridge.org
National Geographic magazines.

Brothers' Helpers
215 Foothill Blvd
La Canada CA 91011
818-949-4338
www.BrothersHelpers.org
Basic toiletries, clothing, shampoo, and toothpaste.

California Wildlife Center
PO Box 2022
Malibu CA 90265
818-222-2658
Canned cat and dog food, cotton balls, coffee cans (large plastic), latex gloves, mesh berry baskets (little plastic), sweatshirts sleeves (for possums to burrow in), and towels.

Call to Protect (The Wireless Foundation)
2555 Bishop Circle West
Dexter MI 48130-1563
888-901-7233
www.DonateaPhone.com
old cell phones

Camp To Belong
P O Box 1146
Marana AZ 85653
303-993-7845
520-413-1395
Art supplies, backpacks, and sleeping bags.

Cancer Research
various locations
800-443-4224
Search Google for Web sites and specific information
General donations will pick up.

Central Christian Church
1001 New Beginnings Dr
Henderson NV 89011
702-735-4004
Food, furniture, material (fabric), notions, and thread.

Children's Hunger Fund
PO Box 7085
Mission Hills CA 91346-7085
818-899-5122 800-708-7589
bbiggers@childrenshungerfund.org
Bar soaps, beans, blankets, cars, clothing, feminine products, glue, notebooks, paper, pencils, pens, stuffed animals, rice, rulers, school supplies, shampoo, soap, sports equipment, staplers, survival items, toothpaste, and toys for boys.

Church that supports a missionary program
various locations
Search Google for Web sites and specific information
Walkers and wheel chairs.

Cinderella Dreams
Cinderella Project (The)
Cinderella's Closet
Cinderella's Trunk
Dress for Success
Enchanted Closet (The)
Fairy Godmother Project
Fairy Godmothers
Fairy Godmothers Inc
Glass Slipper Project (The)
Gowns for Girls
Inside the Dream
My Fairy Godmother
Operation Fairy Dust
Priceless Gown Project
Princess Project (The)
Ruby Room (The)
various locations
Search Google for Web sites and specific information
Bridesmaid and prom dresses.

Clubs-for-Kids
PGA
561-624-8400 ask to be transferred to Section Level
Golf clubs. Contact golf course's pro shop.

Dress for Success
32 East 31st St 7th Floor
New York NY 10016
303-832-1889
212-532-1922
www.dressforsuccess.org/news_media_pr_SOS2007.aspx
Cleaned items on hangers (styles less than five years old): blouses, costume jewelry, handbags, jackets, scarves, shoes, slacks, and suits.

EcoPhones
2828 Anode Ln
Dallas TX 75220
888-326-7466
www.ecophones.com
Recycling cell phones, digital cameras ink jet cartridges and laptop computers. Free shipping.

Excess Access
www.Excessaccess.com
Excess Access Random knickknacks. Got something you don't know what to do with. Matches your items with nonprofit wish lists.

Free Arts for Abused Children
12095 W Washington Blvd Ste 104
Los Angeles CA 90066
310-313-4278
Acrylic paint (water based, 1/2 gallon bottles or larger), baby wipes, bookshelves, canvases, storage containers with lids (clear plastic 16"w x 12"l x 12"h), construction paper, copier paper, decorating materials (buttons, feathers, foam, googley eyes, pipe cleaners, pom poms, sequins, wood shapes), digital camera, disposable cameras, folding chairs, glitter glue, glitter paint, gray sculpting clay, iPod, iPod speakers, jewelry making materials (including fancy beads, fasteners, and wire), paper towels, photo printer, plastic table cloths, postage stamps (27¢ and 42¢), poster board, sandpaper, sharpie brand markers, shelving, sketch books, tempra paint, toilet paper, treasure boxes (small boxes with lids that fit over the entire box), vellum drawing paper, watercolor paper, wooden forks, and wooden spoons.

Friends of the Library
your local library
Search Google for Web sites and specific information
Books.

Gathering Place for Women
1535 High St
Denver CO 80218
303-321-4198
www.the-gatheringplace.org/aboutus.html
Non-perishable food: baby food, beans, canned fruit, canned stews/soups, canned tuna or meats, canned vegetables, coffee, cup-o-soups, pasta, peanut butter, powdered Similac formula, raman noodles, rice, Spagettios, spaghetti sauce, tea, and tuna/hamburger helper. Toiletries: antiperspirant, baby formula, baby lotion, baby shampoo, baby soap, baby wipes, children's socks, conditioner, deodorant, diaper cream, diapers, disposable razors, feminine hygiene supplies, formula, pedialyte, shampoo, sippy cups, soap, toothpaste, and underwear. Storage bins, (plastic 5 to 12 gallon) and school supplies.

Girls Think Tank of San Diego
PO Box 620633
San Diego CA 92162
877-365-3566
www.girlsthinktank.com
girlsthinktank@gmail.com
Backpacks, bags with zippers, blankets, coats, deodorant, large sized clothes (men's and women's XL or above), mini conditioners, mini shampoo, rain gear, shampoos, shaving items, shoes, sleeping bags, soaps, socks, sweatpants, sweatshirts, toiletries, toothbrushes, toothpaste, umbrellas, and warm clothing.

Give the Gift of Sight
4000 Luxottica Pl
Mason OH 45040
800-541-LENS
Eye glasses. Drop off at LensCrafters, Pearle Vision, Sears Optical, Sunglass Hut or Target Optical.

Habitat for Humanity of Greater Los Angeles
17700 S Figueroa St
Gardena CA 90248
310-323-4663
www.shophabitat.org/shophabitat/Materialdonate.htm
Building materials in good, reusable condition: bricks, doors, lumber, and windows. Will pick up.

Harbor Interfaith Shelter - Shelter Partnership
670 W 9th Place
San Pedro CA 90731
310-831-0603
Appliances, clothing, food, and household furniture.

Healing Tree Arts
PO Box 3398
Laguna Hills CA 92654
949-859-9346
877-430-5584
info@healingtreearts.com
Appliances, electronics forestry tools, and eco friendly construction paper.

Hope Chest Thrift Store
4203 N Peck Road
El Monte CA 91732
626-579-3403
www.hopehouse.org/HOPECHESTPAGE.htm
General donations.

HopeLink
Daniele Dreitzer, Executive Direction
178 Westminster Way
Henderson NV 89015
702-566-0576
www.link2hope.org
Non-perishable goods and clothing.

Human Options
419 E 17th St
Costa Mesa CA 92627
949-737-5242
www.HumanOptions.org
Clothing for their store *Classy Second.*

Impact Bay Area
1724 Mandela Pkwy Ste 1
Oakland CA 94607
510-208-0474
www.impactbayarea.org
Blank VHS tapes, boxes of tissue, colored paper, duct tape, DVD-Rs, kitchen garbage bags, liquid hand soap, name tags, padded DVD envelopes and paper towels.

International Book Project
1440 Delaware Avenue
Lexington KY 40505
888-999-2665
Books. Does not accept: books in poor condition (torn, missing pages), encyclopedias, magazines, textbooks copyrighted before 2000.

LA's Prom Closet
www.myspace.com/laspromcloset
laspromcloset@yahoo.com
Prom dresses.

Lions Clubs International
Health and Children's Services
300 W 22nd St
Oak Brook IL 60523-8842
www.lionsclubs.org/EN/content/vision_eyeglass_sight.shtml
eyeglasses@lionsclubs.org
Eye glasses.

Making Memories
12708 SE Stephens St
Portland OR 97233
503-491-8091
Wedding gown.

Mend
10641 N San Fernando Rd
Pacoima CA 91331
818-897-2443
Clothes, computers, medical supplies, and shoes.

National Council of Jewish Women
800-400-6259
www.ncjwla.org
General donations.

National Cristina Foundation
500 W Putnam Ave
Greenwich CT 06830
203-863-9100
www.cristina.org
Computers.

National Furniture Bank Association
Multiple locations nationwide
800-576-0774
dlawrence@Help1Up.org
Furniture.

Nike Reuse-a-Shoe
26755 SW 95th Avenue
Wilsonville OR 97070
800-352-6453
Sneakers (any brand).

On It Foundation
18520 NW 67th Ave Ste 186
Miami, FL 33015
305-945-5889
Computer equipment.

One Warm Coat
PO Box 642850
San Francisco CA 94164
877-663-9276
www.onewarmcoat.org
Coats, ski jackets and sweaters.

Operation Happy Note
122 E Lincoln Ave
Fergus Falls MN 56537
218-736-5541
Musical instruments.

Operation Homefront
PO Box 26747
San Diego CA 92196
866-424-5210
www.operationhomefront.net/socal
Baby items, computers (Pentium III or higher, 650 MHZ), digital cameras, e-trash recycling (cell phones, ink cartridges, toner), furniture, non-perishable foods, and school supplies.

Our Lady of Hope Resident
Attn: Sister Frances
Little Sisters of the Poor
1 Jeanne Jugan Ln
Latham NY 12110
518-785-4551
Small stuffed animals.

P.R.O. (Prescription bottle Recycling Operation)
Jacob Willard
PO Box 269
Barrackville WV 26559
304-363-7789
Millerbre68@aol.com
Prescription bottles. This is a 4-H project working with a free clinic. Contact to see if project is still active. "I recycle prescription bottles and donate to Health Right in Morgantown (free clinic). Please remove the labels."

Play It Again Sports
various locations
Search Google for Web sites and specific information
Sports equipment (golf, baseball, hockey, snow sports, lacrosse) You can sell or donate.

Project Linus
multiple locations
judie.agee@fastq.com
Acrylic yarn, cotton, flannel fabric, fleece, or make a blanket.

Project Night Night
1800 Gough St Ste 5
San Francisco CA 94109
415-310-0360
Baby blankets, children's books and stuffed animals.

Retirement Home
various locations
Search Google for Web sites and specific information
Magazines and greeting cards for craft activities.

Ronald McDonald House
The Pasadena Ronald McDonald House
763 S Pasadena Ave
Pasadena CA 91105
626-585-1588 x 106
Children's books, pantry items, paper products, and pop tabs from cans.

Rosie's Place
889 Harrison Ave
Roxbury MA 02118
617-442-9322
Plus size women's suits (16, 18, 20, 22, 24).

Shared Bread
2005 Flournoy Rd
Manhattan Beach CA 90266
310-545-1631
Blankets, canned foods, hygiene items, and jackets.

SHAWL House
936 S Center St
San Pedro CA 90732
310-521-9310
Clothing and furniture.

Sisters of Charity of Rolling Hills
28600 Palos Verdes Drive East
Rancho Palos Verdes CA 90275
310-831-4101
General donations.

Society of Saint Vincent de Paul
210 North Avenue 21
Los Angeles CA 90031-1792
323-224-6288
http://svdpusa.org
General donations.

South Bay Children's Health Care
410 S Camino Real
Redondo Beach CA 90277
310-316-1212
Dental equipment and supplies.

Standup For Kids
1510 Front St Ste 100
San Diego CA 92101
800-365-4KID
Backpacks, blankets, clothing, food, personal care items and sleeping bags.

Sunnyvale Presbyterian Church's Refugee Outreach Ministry and Catholic Charities of Santa Clara County
1112 S Bernardo Avenue
Sunnyvale CA 94087-2056
408-739-1892
www.svpc.us/refugee_partnership.html
refugee@svpc.us
Basic kitchen supplies, bath towels, bicycles, blankets, bowls, cooking utensils, cutlery, dish towels, dishes, fans, helmets, lamps, pans, plates, pots, sheets, small kitchen tables/chairs, towels, twin size linen, and wall clocks.

Tailored For Success, Inc.
6 Pleasant St Ste 403
Malden MA 02148
781-324-0499
Cleaned items on hangers: women's and men's business suits.

Volunteers of the Burbank Animal Shelter
1150 North Victory Pl
Burbank CA 91502
818-238-3344
www.basv.org/index.html
Cat litter, pet food, and pet grooming supplies.

Wardrobe for Opportunity
570 14th St Ste 5
Oakland CA 94612
510-463-4100
Clean clothing on hangers: belts, coats, handbags, jewelry, plus-sized suits for women and big and tall suits for men, shoes, umbrellas, and unopened cosmetics.

Warm Hearts ~ Warm Babies
PO Box 1266
Brighton CO 80601
info@warmheartswarmbabies.org
Crochet, knit, quilt or sew for infants.

Working Wardrobes
Jerri Rosen Exec. Dir.
11614 Martens River Cir
Fountain Valley CA 92708
714-210-2460
Jewelry, men's shoes, party dresses, and prom dresses.

Product	Where
antiperspirant	Gathering Place for Women
appliances	Healing Tree Arts, Harbor Interfaith Shelter
appliances to recycle	ASBA
art supplies	Camp To Belong
baby: blankets, clothes, diaper cream, diapers, food, formula, items, lotion, pedialyte, powdered similac formula, shampoo, sippy cups, soap, wipes	Blossom Birth, Project Night Night, Operation Homefront, Gathering Place for Women, Free Arts for Abused Children
backpacks	Camp To Belong, Girls Think Tank of San Diego, Standup For Kids
bags with zippers	Girls Think Tank of San Diego
baskets, little plastic mesh berry	California Wildlife Center
belts	Wardrobe for Opportunity
bicycles	Sunnyvale Presbyterian Church's Refugee Outreach
blankets, handmade	Animal Rescue, Animal Shelter, Humane Society, Children's Hunger Fund, Girls Think Tank of San Diego, Shared Bread, Standup For Kids, Warm Hearts ~ Warm Babies, Sunnyvale Presbyterian Church's Refugee Outreach
blouses	Dress for Success
books: children's books; pregnancy, birth, babies, and parenting	Books for Treats, Friends of the Library; International Book Project, Project Night Night, Ronald McDonald House, Blossom Birth
bookshelves	Free Arts for Abused Children
bowls	Free Arts for Abused Children
bricks, doors, lumber, windows, ceiling fans	ANEW, Habitat for Humanity
building materials	Habitat for Humanity
camera, digital	Operation Homefront, Free Arts for Abused Children
camera, digital to recycle	EcoPhones
camera, disposable	Free Arts for Abused Children
canvases	Free Arts for Abused Children
cards, greeting	Retirement home
carpet	ANEW
cars	Children's Hunger Fund
cat litter	Volunteers of the Burbank Animal Shelter
cell phones to recycle	Call To Protect, EcoPhones, Operation Homefront
chairs, folding	Free Arts for Abused Children
clay, gray sculpting	Free Arts for Abused Children
cleaning supplies	Animal Rescue, Animal Shelter, Humane Society
clothes/clothing	1736 Family Crisis Center Shelter Partnership, Inc.; Brothers' Helpers; HopeLink; Human Options, SHAWL House, Children's Hunger Fund, Harbor Interfaith Shelter, Girls Think Tank of San Diego, Mend, Standup For Kids
coats, jackets, ski jackets	One Warm Coat, Dress for Success, Girls Think Tank of San Diego, Shared Bread, Wardrobe for Opportunity
coffee	Gathering Place for Women
coffee cans, large plastic	California Wildlife Center
computer equipment; computers (Pentium III or higher, 650 Mhz)	National Cristina Foundation; On It Foundation, Mend, Operation Homefront
computers and computers laptop to recycle	ASBA, EcoPhones
conditioner, mini conditioners	Girls Think Tank of San Diego, Gathering Place for Women
cooking utensils	Sunnyvale Presbyterian Church's Refugee Outreach
cosmetics unopened	Wardrobe for Opportunity
costumes	Community theater, High school drama department
cotton	Project Linus
cotton balls	California Wildlife Center
cutlery	Sunnyvale Presbyterian Church's Refugee Outreach
decorating materials (buttons, feathers, foam, googley eyes, pipe cleaners, pom poms, sequins, wood shapes)	Free Arts for Abused Children
dental equipment and supplies	South Bay Children's Health Care
deodorant	Girls Think Tank of San Diego, Gathering Place for Women
dishes	Sunnyvale Presbyterian Church's Refugee Outreach
dresses: bridesmaid, prom and party	Cinderella Dreams, Cinderella Project (The), Cinderella's Closet, Cinderella's Trunk, Dress for Success, Enchanted Closet (The), Fairy

Product	Where
	Godmother Project, Fairy Godmothers, Fairy Godmothers Inc, Glass Slipper Project (The), Gowns for Girls, Inside the Dream, My Fairy Godmother, Operation Fairy Dust, Priceless Gown Project, Princess Project (The), Ruby Room (The), Working Wardrobes, LA's Prom Closet
duct tape	Impact Bay Area
DVD-Rs	Impact Bay Area
DVDS	Blossom Birth
electronics, small	ASBA
envelopes, padded DVD	Impact Bay Area
eye glasses	Give the Gift of Sight, Lions Clubs International
fabric, flannel	Central Christian Church, Project Linus
fans	Sunnyvale Presbyterian Church's Refugee Outreach
feminine hygiene supplies	Children's Hunger Fund, Shared Bread, Gathering Place for Women
fleece	Project Linus
food, pantry items and non-perishable foods: beans; canned foods; canned fruit; canned stews/soups; canned tuna or meats; canned vegetables; cup-o-soups; tuna/hamburger helper; raman noodles, rice, spagettios, spaghetti sauce, tea, pasta, peanut butter	Central Christian Church; Postal Carrier; HopeLink, Children's Hunger Fund, Harbor Interfaith Shelter, Operation Homefront, Shared Bread, Standup For Kids, Ronald McDonald House, Gathering Place for Women
forks wooden	Free Arts for Abused Children
general donations	Cancer Research, Hope Chest Thrift Store, Society of Saint Vincent de Paul
glue, glitter glue	Children's Hunger Fund, Free Arts for Abused Children
handbags	Dress for Success, Wardrobe for Opportunity
hangers	Local dry cleaner
hardware	ANEW
hearing aids	Lion Clubs
helmets	Sunnyvale Presbyterian Church's Refugee Outreach
furniture, household furniture	ANEW, National Furniture Bank Association, SHAWL House, Harbor Interfaith Shelter, Central Christian Church; Operation Homefront
household items	1736 Family Crisis Center Shelter Partnership, Inc.
ink jet cartridges to recycle	EcoPhones, Operation Homefront
iPod and iPod speakers	Free Arts for Abused Children
jewelry making materials (fancy beads, fasteners, wire)	Free Arts for Abused Children
jewelry, costume jewelry	Dress for Success, Working Wardrobes, Wardrobe for Opportunity
kitchen garbage bags	Impact Bay Area
kitchen supplies	Sunnyvale Presbyterian Church's Refugee Outreach
kitchen tables and chairs small	Sunnyvale Presbyterian Church's Refugee Outreach
knickknacks	Excess Access
lamps	Sunnyvale Presbyterian Church's Refugee Outreach
latex gloves	California Wildlife Center
magazines	Retirement home
maternity clothes	Blossom Birth
medical supplies	Mend
musical instruments	Local public school music teachers, Operation Happy Note
name tags	Impact Bay Area
National Geographic magazines	Books for the Barrios, Bridge to Asia
notebooks (paper)	Children's Hunger Fund
notions	Central Christian Church
paint acrylic (water based, 1/2 gallon bottles or larger); paint glitter; paint tempra	Free Arts for Abused Children
pans	Sunnyvale Presbyterian Church's Refugee Outreach
paper products	Ronald McDonald House
paper: watercolor; vellum drawing; colored, construction, copier	Children's Hunger Fund, Impact Bay Area, Healing Tree Arts, Free Arts for Abused Children
peanuts (packing)	Most pack and ship places will take them
pencils	Children's Hunger Fund
pens, Sharpies	Children's Hunger Fund, Free Arts for Abused Children
personal care items	Standup For Kids
pet supplies and pet grooming supplies	Volunteers of the Burbank Animal Shelter, Animal shelters,

Product	Where
	Veterinarians, Kennels, Animal hospitals
pets: canned cat and dog food, pet food	California Wildlife Center, Volunteers of the Burbank Animal Shelter
storage containers with lids (plastic clear 16"w x 12"l x 12"h); storage bins (plastic 5 to 12 gallon)	Free Arts for Abused Children
plates	Sunnyvale Presbyterian Church's Refugee Outreach
plus-sized suits for women (16, 18, 20, 22, 24)	
big and tall suits for men	Rosie's Place, Wardrobe for Opportunity, Girls Think Tank of San Diego, Wardrobe for Opportunity
pop tabs (pull tabs)	Ronald McDonald House
postage stamps (postcard and first-class)	Free Arts for Abused Children
poster board	Free Arts for Abused Children
pots	Sunnyvale Presbyterian Church's Refugee Outreach
prescription bottles	P.R.O. (Prescription bottle Recycling Operation)
printer, photo	Free Arts for Abused Children
rain gear	Girls Think Tank of San Diego
razors, disposable	Gathering Place for Women
rulers	Children's Hunger Fund
sandpaper	Free Arts for Abused Children
scarves	Dress for Success
school supplies	Operation Homefront, Gathering Place for Women
shampoo, shampoos (little)	Brothers' Helpers, Children's Hunger Fund, Gathering Place for Women, Women's shelters, Girls Think Tank of San Diego
Sharpie brand markers	Free Arts for Abused Children
shaving items	Girls Think Tank of San Diego
sheets (linens), twin size	Animal Rescue, Animal Shelter, Humane Society, Sunnyvale Presbyterian Church's Refugee Outreach
shelving	Free Arts for Abused Children
shoes; men's	Dress for Success, Girls Think Tank of San Diego, Mend, Working Wardrobes, Wardrobe for Opportunity
sketch books	Free Arts for Abused Children
slacks	Dress for Success
sleeping bags	Camp To Belong, Girls Think Tank of San Diego, Standup For Kids
sneakers	Nike Reuse-a-Shoe
soap: liquid hand, bar, little soaps	Children's Hunger Fund, Girls Think Tank of San Diego, Impact Bay Area, Gathering Place for Women
socks, children's	Girls Think Tank of San Diego, Gathering Place for Women
spoons wooden	Free Arts for Abused Children
sports equipment: golf, baseball, hockey, snow sports, lacrosse	School programs, Youth centers, Boys & Girls club, Police Athletic League, Clubs-for-Kids PGA, Play It Again Sports, Children's Hunger Fund
staplers	Children's Hunger Fund
stuffed animals, small, plush	Our Lady of Hope Resident, Project Night Night, Children's Hunger Fund
suits: women's and men's business	Dress for Success, Tailored For Success, Inc.
survival items	Children's Hunger Fund
sweaters	One Warm Coat
sweatpants and sweatshirts	Girls Think Tank of San Diego
sweatshirts sleeves (for possums to burrow in)	California Wildlife Center
table cloths, plastic	Free Arts for Abused Children
thread	Central Christian Church
tissue	Impact Bay Area
toilet paper	Free Arts for Abused Children
toiletries	Brothers' Helpers, Girls Think Tank of San Diego
toner cartiages to recycle	Operation Homefront
toothpaste	Brothers' Helpers, Children's Hunger Fund, Girls Think Tank of San Diego, Gathering Place for Women
towels: paper, bath, dish	Animal Rescue; Animal Shelter; Humane Society; California Wildlife Center, Impact Bay Area, Sunnyvale Presbyterian Church's Refugee Outreach, Free Arts for Abused Children
toys, boys	1736 Family Crisis Center Shelter Partnership, Inc., Children's

Product	Where
	Hunger Fund
treasure boxes (small boxes with lids that fit over the entire box)	Free Arts for Abused Children
t-shirts	Animal Rescue; Animal Shelter; Humane Society
TV to recycle	ASBA
Umbrellas	Girls Think Tank of San Diego, Wardrobe for Opportunity
underwear	Gathering Place for Women
vases	Clean ones to local hospital gift store or florist
VHS tapes, blank	Impact Bay Area
videos, children	Ronald McDonald House; Friends of the Library
walkers	Church that supports a missionary program
wall clocks	Sunnyvale Presbyterian Church's Refugee Outreach
wedding gown	Making Memories
wheel chairs	Church that supports a missionary program
women's clothing see also clothing, suites and plus-sized	Dress for Success
yarn, acrylic	Project Linus

Household Hazardous Waste (HHW) is any product labeled toxic, poisonous, corrosive, flammable, combustible or irritant, including lawn and garden-care products, paint and paint-related products, automotive fluids and batteries, beauty products and medicines, household cleaners and other products such as shoe polish, and glue.

Your Toolbox

What should you bring with you when you arrive at your client? You will develop your own bag of must haves must here are some of mine. Latex gloves, Ziploc bags (various sizes), camera (before and after photos), label maker, sticky notes, hand lotion, Sharpie and highlighters, measuring tape (3-5' from Container Store $2.99) and calculator.

Square boxes: dishpan (great for papers—in basket); kitty litter pan (great for bigger projects—income taxes, legal papers, craft projects); check boxes (great for organizing the supply closet); Velveeta cheese boxes (great for organizing the supply closet's larger items).

I have found Moving Men to be very helpful. I can move a fully loaded bookcase or file cabinet with them. They are often found at Home Depot or drug stores for about $10. Don't get the other brand, they just don't stand up as long.

I don't like to BUY a lot of items. I have found most clients have already gone out and purchased a bunch of stuff in an effort to get organized. **REPURPOSE** what they already have.

Creating the BUSINESS

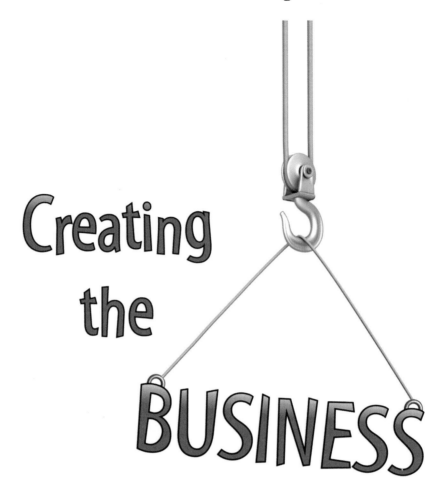

Section 2: Creating the Business

As a Professional Organizer, you need to establish the business. Those pesky little things that you might not know you need to do.

There are several types of business structures. They are: sole proprietor, partnership, corporation, nonprofit, and Limited Liability Company. Some of these structures are formed at the county level and some at the state level.

Sole Proprietorship

A sole proprietorship is an unincorporated business that is owned by one individual (or a married couple). It is the simplest form of business organization.

For most individuals, a sole proprietorship is the type of business to set up. It's easy and uncomplicated. You are the business and the business is you. Business income and expenses are reported on your personal income taxes.

Guidelines whether to create a sole proprietorship are:

- You (or your spouse) have very few assets to protect.
- The type of business you're going into isn't prone to lawsuits.
- You're not planning to sell the business (when you retire, the business retires).
- You're not planning to have many (if any) employees.

Sole proprietor files a Schedule C along with the regular 1040 for to report the business income or loss.

You are called an owner of a sole proprietorship.

Business Name

What you call your business is not as important as the products you sell. Clients are buying the products, not the name. If you plan to sell the business in the future, the value of the business is higher if the name of the business does not contain your name.

For some people, deciding on the name of their company is easy. For others, giving birth to a child is easier. Here are three things to consider when choosing your company name.

1. Is it possible to include the name of what you are selling in the name of the company?
2. Is the name of your business too broad?
3. Is the name of your business too narrow? If you were to choose another product or service, would the name be outdated? Today, company names with dot com seem to be outdated.

4. Research the name you have in mind using Google or some other search engine. How many other companies have the same name or something close? You want people to remember your name, but you don't want them going to the competition or to another vendor.

Domain Name (URL)

One of the most important aspects of your business, after creating your business name, is to link that business name with your domain name or URL (Universal Resource Locator) on the Internet.

Get a URL (name) for your site that makes sense. It should be uniquely yours and something that people will remember. Do your best to keep it fewer than 15 characters. The longer the URL is, the more possibilities there are for clients to mistype it. If they misspell your URL, they will never find you.

To make your life easier, go to our Web site, www.RoundsMiller.com, click onto the Affiliate Services, look for the Web site hosting & domain names (either 1 and 1; or Go Daddy). Select either 1and1 or GoDaddy. Either of these web hosting companies are good and have been around for years.

Domain name registration can be accomplished by paying an annual fee to Network Solutions (www.NetworkSolutions.com), either directly or through a broker/dealer. Go to www.WhoIs.net research the name in a matter of minutes.

High quality, low-cost domain name availability and Web site hosting is at www.GoDaddy.com or www.1and1.com. Each has a search engine that will help you search what is available. You can register the domain name there or shop for a better rate.

The fees range from $2 to $35 per year depending on who is brokering the process. Here are some other sites that offer reduced rates on domain name registration: www.DomainDirect.com, www.enom.com, www.Hover.com, www.APlusNet.com, www.Register.com and www.RegSelect.com.

Domain name kidnapping is a practice that occurs when unscrupulous Web site designers seek a way to make additional money from you, or they want to create an insurance policy against you changing designers. This is how it could happen: you request that the Web site developer register your domain name. The request is a valid and sound business practice as long as the developer registers the domain name in your name and passes the registration and billing along to you. When this process is followed, you get to use the domain name and have paid the developer for registering the name.

The problem occurs when the developer registers the name to his organization instead of yours and doesn't tell you. The kidnapping process occurs if you decide to terminate the services of the developer. At this point, the unscrupulous developer will announce that he owns the domain name, then he charges you an exorbitant amount of money (sometimes thousands of dollars) to change the registration to you.

The primary problem with domain name kidnapping is that although it's unethical, it isn't technically illegal. To prevent your domain name from being kidnapped, be conscientious and insist that you are the actual registrant for your domain name and that you receive the annual invoices from Network Solutions.

Doing Business As (DBA)—Fictitious Business Name Statement

Names that suggest the existence of additional owners must be registered as fictitious business names. This is also known as filing a DBA (Doing Business As) or a Fictitious Name Statement (FNS). A fictitious name statement is the lowest form of registration. The registration is either accomplished at the county clerk's office or with the secretary of state. Not all counties require a doing business (fictitious business name) nor do all states.

At the county level, this is handled by the county clerk, county recorder or country clerk/recorder's office.

The types of business structures that can file a Fictitious Business Name are: an individual, a corporation, a limited partnership, a general partnership, a trust, husband and wife, a limited liability company, and/or state or local registered domestic partners. You can file more than one DBA at a time.

Before you fill out the DBA, here is what you need to know. Who is filing for a DBA, what is the address and in what publication will the DBA be published (you don't have to know the answer at the time of filing but it must be done within 30 days of filing. Typically, send the original and three copies of the form (one certified copy is for the bank, one copy is for the newspaper, and one copy is for your record), a self-addressed stamped envelope to ensure a prompt return of your copies, and payment. You may pay by check (personal, company, bank, or cashiers), money order or traveler's checks.

The county clerk's office is only a repository of fictitious business name statements. They don't research the business name. They don't approve or disapprove the name, or check for similarities or duplications among DBA's. Many states do not have a state-wide database. The filing of a fictitious business name statement does not guarantee exclusive use of that name. Check with the Secretary of State's (California www.:ss.ca.gov/business/corp/corporate.htm) to check if there is a corporation with your name or the US Patent and Trademark Office (www.USPTO).

The first part is filing the DBA with the county clerk; the second part is publishing it in a newspaper.

Filing

There are four different ways that you can file a DBA.

1. The simplest way to accomplish the filing of a DBA is to contact your local newspaper. The newspaper has the forms and the knowledge of what needs to be done and how to do it. You fill out the paperwork and the newspaper processes the statement to the county clerk. Check around for the newspaper with the cheapest rates. In our research, we haven't found information about filing a DBA on the newspaper's Web site.

2. Go to the county clerk's office. You may have to pass by some people waiting there. If they offer to give you directions and you say the clerk's office, they will give you

the directions and a flyer for publication of the notice in their publication. After you file with the county clerk's office, you must publish the notice in a newspaper.

3. Call the county clerk and ask that the forms be mailed to you. Return the completed statement to the clerk along with the fee for filing the statement. Then newspapers will send you their flyers. After you file with the county clerk's office, you must publish the notice in a newspaper.

4. Go online. Some counties have online forms for you to fill out. Most counties have PDF versions of the forms for you to mail back. Then newspapers (some you have never heard of) will send you their flyers. After you file with the county clerk's office, you must publish the notice in a newspaper.

   www.LegalZoom.com is a popular Web site that many people use for obtaining all of the legal forms you'll need in your business.

   If you do an Internet search for filing a DBA, be careful. You will get Web sites that charge a lot and scare you by telling you all the things that you have to do. Use these words to search: fictitious business name (FBN) and your county name/state [Fictitious Business Name McLeod County]. Look for Web sites that seem like they belong to the county, the county clerk/recorder or the state. Not a legal firm or company.

Publishing
Within 30 days after filing a DBA, a copy of the statement must be published in a newspaper of general circulation in the county in which the principal place of business is located. The notice must appear once per week for four successive weeks with at least five days between the notices.

An affidavit of the published filing must be sent to the county clerk within 30 days after the publication.

If your county has no publication, then the county of the state capital usually is where you must publish the notice.

Re-Filing
A fictitious name statement expires five years from the date it was filed. If there have been no changes (the individuals are the same) the re-filing fee is less than the original filing or there may be no additional fee if filed within 40 days or expiration. After 40 days, you will need to file again.

If there has been any change in the residence address of a registered owner, you need to notify the Clerk.

It is your responsibility to re-file before the five years expires. However, we have noticed that newspapers whose primary purpose is filing DBA's will notify you.

Because we give seminars primarily in Arizona, California, and Nevada, we are going to outline the DBA process in those states. Your local SBA (www.SBA.gov) is a good place for these types of answers.

Arizona
Arizona does not require that you have a DBA. However if you would like to, you can do so with the Secretary of State (www.AZSoS.gov) for $10.

California
Alameda County
Alameda County Clerk-Recorder's Office, 1106 Madison Street, Oakland, CA 94607. The fee is $29 for the first business name and $7 for each additional business name. You can research Fictitious Business Names online at no charge. www.acgov.org/index.htm.

Fresno County
Go to www.Co.fresno.ca.us or call 559-488-3246. The fee is $35 for the first business name and $7 for each additional business name.

Kern County
County Clerk of Kern County, 1115 Truxtun Avenue, Bakersfield, CA 93301 661-868-3588. www.co.kern.ca.us/ctyclerk/dba/default.asp. The fee is $30 for the first business name and $6 for each additional business name.

Los Angeles County
The cheapest for Los Angeles County is Paramount Journal (800-540-1870) who will publish your DBA for $58 + $23 ($81) to the country clerk. Or go to www.lavote.net/CLERK/Business_Name.cfm. The fee is $23 for the first business name and $4 for each additional business name.

Monterey County
Monterey County Clerk, PO Box 29, Salinas, CA 93902, 831-755-5450 to speak with a staff member. www.co.monterey.ca.us/Recorder/ficbusnm.htm. The fee is $30 for the first business name and $7 for each additional business name.

Napa County
Napa County Recorder/Clerk PO Box 298, Napa CA 94559-0298, clerk@co.napa.ca.us, www.co.napa.ca.us/GOV/Departments/DeptPage.asp?DID=28000&LID=622 707-253-4247 The fee is $30 for the first business name and $6 for each additional business name.

Orange County
Orange County, go to www.ocrecorder.com/FBNFiling.asp. The fee is $27 for the first business name. The Web site has a list of newspapers where you can file. The cheapest we have found is $20 with a coupon at 949-589-9990.

Riverside County
Fictitious Business Name Statement (ACR 500) E-Form. PO Box 751, Riverside CA 92502-0751 or 82-675 Hwy 111 Room 113, Indio CA 92201 951-486-7000. http://riverside.asrclkrec.com. The fee is $35 for the first business name and $7 for each additional business name.

Sacramento County
Business License Unit of the Department of Finance, 700 H Street, Room 1710, Sacramento, CA 95814. www.finance.saccounty.net/Tax/FBNGeneral.asp#. The fee is $25 for the first business name and $5 for each additional business name.

San Bernardino County
Auditor/Controller-Recorder, 222 West Hospitality Lane, San Bernardino, CA 92415-0022 909-386-8970 www.co.san-bernardino.ca.us/acr/RecSearch.htm. The fee is $40 for the first business name and $10 for each additional business name.

San Diego County
San Diego Recorder/County Clerk, PO Box 121750, San Diego, CA 92112-1750 http://arcc.co.san-diego.ca.us/arcc/services/fbn_info.aspx Attn: FBN. The fee is $30 for the first business name and $5 for each additional business name.

San Mateo County
www.smcare.org/clerk/fictitious The fee is $34 for the first business name and $5 for each additional business name.

Santa Barbara County
www.sbcvote.com/ClerkRecorder/FictitiousBusinessName.aspx#text The fee is $33 for the first business name and $6 for each additional business name.

Solano County
County Clerk, 675 Texas St, Ste 1900, Fairfield CA 94533-6337 707-784-7510. The fee is $24 for the first business name and $5 for each additional business name.

Sonoma County
Sonoma County Clerk, 2300 County Center Drive, Ste. B-177, Santa Rosa, CA 95403 707-565-3700 or 707-565-3800. The fee is $34 for the first business name and $7 for each additional business name.

Stanislaus County
County Clerk, PO Box 1670, 1021 I St Ste 101, Modesto CA 95353 209-525-5250. The fee is $34 for the first business name and $7 for each additional business name.

Ventura County
For Ventura County, go to http://recorder.countyofventura.org/clerk.htm. The fee is $53. The fee is $53 for the first business name and $10 for each additional business name.

Yuba County
County Recorder, 915 8th St Ste 107, Marysville, CA 95901. The fee is $30 for the first business name and $5 for each additional business name.

Nevada
Clark County
A Fictitious FIRM Name DBA is required for all businesses that plan to use a name different than their legal or corporate name. County Clerk, Attn: FFN, PO Box 551604, Las Vegas, NV 89155-1604. You can file online using www.NevadaTax.nv.gov/web. The fee is $20 and the renewal is $20.

Partnership

Going into business with another individual other than your spouse is a partnership. Although partnerships are easy to start, consider a formal partnership agreement. In a partnership, the other person can create liabilities (put you in debt) and has access to assets—with or without your knowledge or consent.

Partnerships are good when one individual has skills or resources that the other doesn't (opposites attract) or the two of you have a commonality (values, vision and skills) that encourages you to join forces. On the other hand, in a partnership there are often feelings of an inequitable situation. One partner is doing more work, contributing more money, taking out more money than the other partner. This is why you want a partnership agreement.

When creating a partnership, what the partners are contributing can be money, time or resources. One way to be equitable in a partnership, is when one partner wants to take money out, the other partner(s) get an equal amount. So if someone is requesting $10, the cost to the business is $20.

Contact a prepaid legal service, and inquire if this is one of the services they offer. Go to our Web site (www.RoundsMiller.com), click on the link for more information about these services. Or go to your local library and reference Nolo Press's (www.Nolo.com) book Form a Partnership. Many office supply stores carry Nolo Press books and generic legal forms. Many people have commented that they have used www.LegalZoom.com. Our local library's Web site has usable legal forms for free.

A partnership files an IRS Form 1065. The partnership profit or loss is reported on IRS Form K1, and the profit's tax or business loss is reported onto each partner's individual 1040 income tax return.

You are called a partner owner in a partnership.

Corporation

A corporation is an incorporated business that is owned by an individual or individuals. It is like giving birth because once you form a corporation; it has a life separate from you.

Guidelines whether to create a corporation are:

1. You (or your spouse) have assets to protect.

2. The type of business you're going into is prone to lawsuits. The advantage of a corporation is that a corporation stands alone (corporate veil). This means that if you are sued, it's the corporation that gets sued. Your personal assets are still protected.

3. You're planning to sell or go public with the business.

4. You're planning to have employees.

Disadvantages of creating a corporation for a one-business business:

1. If you want a salary, the corporation pays you a salary. At the end of the year, you pay income tax on your salary. So the same money is taxed twice—once through the corporation taxes and once through your personal income taxes.

2. The minimum state tax that a corporation pays is around $800. Even if the corporation doesn't do any business this year, you would still need to pay the $800.

3. The corporation has to be acting like a corporation—you must follow the rules (issuing stocks, and corporate minutes).

The Secretary of State is where you incorporate in your state. Contact this office for specifics.

You are called an officer of a corporation.

There are different types of corporations. They include a C Corp, a Subchapter S Corporation, an LLC, a nonprofit corporation and foreign corporation.

Business Addresses

Depending upon your situation and your circumstances, there are several options for your business address.

Home Address

Instead of spending your money on office space, your home can also function as your business office. You may want to create the image that you are operating as a business—not a hobby. Put Suite 301 on your house or change Apartment 101 to Suite 101. If you live within a homeowners association, it may have restrictions. Check your CC&R (covenants, conditions, and restrictions) for clarification.

Office or Professional Suites

These suites are small offices rented by the month, day, or hour. Suites are a nice way to have people stop by your office without inviting them to your home. They provide conference rooms and a receptionist to greet clients and answer the telephone. In addition, they often offer a full range of secretarial services.

Post Office Box

A popular choice for start-up, home-based, mail order and Internet businesses is renting a Post Office box. The Post Office rental for a box is about $48/$76/$136 per year (small/medium/large). Check the rates in your area.

Private Mailboxes (PMB)

An alternative to a Post Office box is a private mailbox. The most popular of these franchises is The UPS Store (formerly Mail Boxes, Etc.). Usually these addresses begin with the street address, followed by the unit—904 Silver Spur Road, #807 PMB 103. The box is only 3"x5"x15". These suites rent for $15/$20/$25 per month. Check the rates in your area.

Because private mailboxes are not authorized substations of the USPS, they cannot use the words Post Office. Suite 807, Box 332, Penthouse Suite, or 2nd Floor could all be used. Contact the owner of the private mailbox and work out the desired wording.

What type of business structure you want to be is entirely up to you. They all have their pros and cons. Asking people what you should do may not be your best course. Think about what you want the business to be. If it is just a hobby type, then a sole proprietorship is just fine. To get the best use of your money, a sole proprietorship and taking as many home office expenses as possible would be a good way to go. If you want to protect yourself and your money, then a corporation may be the direction to take. If you want another person's support, consider a partnership. The decision is yours.

Independent Contractors

As an independent contractor, the payment that you receive is in gross dollars. The client doesn't take out any taxes. You become responsible for taxes, retirement and insurance. Just because you say you're an independent contractor, doesn't always make you an independent contractor.

The determination of whether an individual who performs services for another is performing services in the capacity of an employee, as opposed to services in the capacity of an independent contractor, carries with it significant federal tax consequences.

If you are employed, the employer:

Must withhold income taxes from the wages paid to employees.

- Must withhold FICA taxes from employees' wages.
- Is required to match the amount of withheld FICA taxes.

Must pay FICA and FUTA taxes on wages paid to employees, subject to credits for unemployment tax payments made into a state unemployment fund.

As an independent contractor:

- Your payment is not subject to neither income nor Social Security taxes withholdings.
- The client is not required to pay its share of FICA taxes or to pay FUTA taxes.
- You will pay the full amount of your Social Security taxes in the form of self-employment taxes.
- You are generally not entitled to protection from discrimination under either the Civil Rights Act of 1964 or the Age Discrimination in Employment Act of 1986.
- You do not receive rights relating to compensation provided by the Fair Labor Standards Act.

- You are not entitled to certain rights under the Occupational Safety and Health Act of 1970.

- Under the common-law test, a worker is an employee if the employer has a right to direct and control when, where, and how the worker performs the tasks. The employer need not exercise control: it is sufficient that the employer has the right to do so.

- The Internal Revenue Service has adopted 20 common-law factors to determine whether the requisite control or right to control exists to establish an employer-employee relationship. The IRS has not given any indication as to the weight to be assigned each of the various factors; however, there is an emphasis on the general notion of control.

The 20 factors are the extent to which:

❒ The employer instructs the worker on how to complete the task.

❒ The employer trains the worker.

❒ The employer sets the order or sequence of work completion.

❒ The employer pays the worker's business and/or travel expenses.

❒ The employer furnishes the worker's tools or materials.

❒ The employer has the right to discharge the worker.

❒ The worker is integrated into the employer's business.

❒ The worker renders his or her services personally.

❒ The worker works on the employer's premises.

❒ The worker reports orally or in writing.

❒ The worker is paid an hourly, weekly, or monthly salary.

❒ The worker does not have a significant investment in the tools or machinery.

❒ The worker has no potential to realize a significant profit or loss.

❒ The worker may work for others simultaneously.

❒ The worker may hire, fire, supervise, or pay assistance.

❒ The worker may make services available to the general public.

❒ The worker has the right to terminate the relationship.

❒ There is a continuing relationship.

- ❒ There are set hours of work.
- ❒ Full-time work is required.

Since all of these factors may not be pertinent in any given situation, and since all of them may not support the same result, commentators describe the following seven factors as the most important:

- ❒ The degree of control exercised by the principal over the details of the work.
- ❒ Which party invests in the facilities used in the work?
- ❒ The opportunity of the worker for profit or loss.
- ❒ Whether the principal has a right to discharge the worker.
- ❒ Whether the work is part of the principal's regular business.
- ❒ The permanency of the relationship.
- ❒ The type of relationship that the principal and worker believe they are creating.

A quick check list of things you need as an independent consultant:

- ❒ EIN Employer Identification Number
- ❒ Business license (if your city, county or state requires it)
- ❒ Business bank account (checking or savings or both)
- ❒ Business card with business contact information
- ❒ Business letterhead with business contact information
- ❒ Health insurance

If you have any questions about whether or not you are an independent contractor, talk with your CPA or call the state. The state is interested in working with you to determine your status. They have a form (Determination of Employment Work Status for Purposes of State Employment Taxes and Personal Income Tax Withholding) which will help in the determination of whether you are operating as an independent contractor.

Trademark

Because of the amount of advertising, promotion, publicity, and the subsequent reputation that is connected with goods and services, trademarks tend to become the identity under which people recognize and purchase a particular line of goods or services.

You will need to provide the US Patent and Trademark Office

(www.USPTO.gov) with five samples of the mark as it is used. A supply of samples of the mark, logo, package, and letterhead will suffice.

The ™ (trademark) may be placed on any logo, name, slogan, etc. as fair warning to others in the trade that you are using this as your trademark.

The SM (service mark) is usually placed on a logo or other device for firms that are dealing with a service rather than a product. The rights, restrictions, and cautions are the same as when using the ™. Molly Maid is a service mark as they come in and clean your house!

The ® (registered mark) is allowed on a mark only after the mark has been officially approved and granted by the US Patent and Trademark Office.

As a result, the trademark may become as valuable as, or even more valuable than, the goods or services it represents.

A trademark: is a word, symbol, slogan, or even a distinctive sound that identifies and distinguishes the goods and services of one party from those of another?

- Takes 6-13 months to be granted, depending on the category selected and the backlog of work. There are 34 classes of goods and 8 classes of services that can be trademarked. It's possible to register the same name in different classes of goods or services.

- Is granted for a period of 10 years and is renewable, as long as the mark is maintained in an active status.

- Costs $375 (electronic filing) per submission, not including charges for the artwork and forms.

- Has a maintenance fee of about $350.

If either the name or the graphic portion of the trademark is deceptively similar to another trademark in the same category, the US Patent and Trademark Office may deny the registration due to its similarity.

A preliminary search can be run by a patent agent, patent attorney, or the US Patent and Trademark Room of a patent library to determine if the mark is available or taken. Many of the libraries offer the Trademark Search service for a minimal fee. The Pasadena City Library (626-405-4052) is one example.

If you are interested in more information on this topic, you may want to purchase Trademarks and Copyrights for the Clueless. Details are available in the back of this book.

Insurance

Insurance comes in many forms and sizes. Sometimes it is appropriate for a start-up, home-based and Professional Organizers. To help you better understand what an agent has to offer, here are some easy descriptions of the different types of insurance.

In John T. Reed's book *How to Manage Residential Property for Maximum Cash Flow*, he says, "An insurance policy is not a lottery ticket. It's not a way of making money by 'cashing in' when you have a loss." The purpose of insurance is to help you get the business back operational, not to give a handout.

The average premiums and coverages listed here are guidelines and may not be applicable to your situation or state. These figures are based on the following composite: a male, age 38 and in good health, married with children, living in a large metropolitan area, who is a sole proprietor working from home in a service-related business—such as a computer consultant—and who owns $5,000 to $7,000 of business property.

Auto Insurance

Auto insurance covers the loss of business property in the car and the costs of accidents when you or someone on your behalf is driving the car for business purposes. When needed: if you use the car for business purposes other than driving to and from work, especially if you transport equipment or merchandise in the car. Estimated cost of average coverage: $1,600 per year (includes regular accident coverage). If you drive a minimum number of miles, you may be able to be placed in a lower-risk category and pay lower premiums.

Ask if using your vehicle while conducting your business is covered under your current auto insurance. It may be, it may not be. Have the talk with your agent before anything happens. Be informed.

Homeowners or Renters Insurance

This is one of the most popular forms of personal insurance on the market. The typical homeowner's policy has two main sections: Section I covers your property, and Section II provides personal liability coverage, which covers you in case of lawsuits arising from things that happen on your property. Almost anyone who owns or leases property should have this type of insurance. It is often required by lenders in order to obtain a mortgage.

A standard renter's policy protects your personal property in many cases of theft or damage and may pay for temporary living expenses if your property is damaged so seriously that you can't live in it. It can also protect you from personal liability.

Generally, for a couple hundred dollars a year, you can get renters or homeowners insurance. Check the wording to see if it covers replacement value (the cost of replacing the item new) or current or actual value (the garage sale price).

A rider is an attachment to a policy that modifies its conditions by expanding or restricting benefits or excluding certain conditions from coverage. Start with homeowners or renters insurance and then add the items below as additional riders to the policy. This is usually cheaper than just getting the type of insurance coverage by themselves.

Check your policy to see if you damage (break) something of your clients if the policy would cover it?

Business-Property Insurance

This protects you from damage or loss to the business property. When needed: if you have any equipment in your home office that is used for business purposes. Estimated cost of average coverage: $50 per year for $5,000 to $7,000 of equipment (as a rider to the homeowner's policy).

Discounts on property insurance rates are sometimes available if you protect your home as follows: fire and smoke alarms, or smoke, heat, or ion detectors approved by Underwriter's Laboratory; dead bolt locks on exterior doors, and home security systems.

To protect your home office from fire and burglary, have the local police and fire departments perform a free inspection. They may recommend additional fire alarms, more secure locks, and perimeter burglar alarms.

Computer Insurance

Computer insurance covers damage to the computer hardware, software, and data. When needed: when computer-related losses are not adequately covered under your property- or small-business insurance policies. Estimated cost of average coverage: $89 per year for $5,000 to $8,000 coverage; $109 per year for $8,000 to $11,000 coverage; $129 per year for $11,000 to $14,000 coverage.

The computer insurance on your homeowner's policy is limited, or you have to pay for a separate rider and there is still a small limit. Check what coverage you actually will have. Many times what you want covered and what you think is covered won't actually be covered.

Computer insurance companies have not been around long. Check out the companies thoroughly. Ask some of your colleagues and find out who they are using.

General Liability Insurance

General liability is primarily concerned with losses caused by negligent acts, bodily injury, property damage on the premises of a business, injury from a product manufactured, or injury occurring in the general operation of a business. When needed: if you do some portion of your work on someone else's premises. Estimated cost of average coverage: included as part of small business insurance; otherwise, about $200 per year.

If you join NAPO, inquire about their liability insurance group coverage.

Liability Insurance

These cover costs of injuries that occur on the property to business-related visitors. When needed: if you ever have delivery people or clients come to your home. Estimated cost of average coverage: $20 per year for $500,000 of coverage (when added as a rider to homeowner's policy).

Malpractice or Errors and Omissions Insurance

These insure against claims or damages that arise out of the services or products you offer. When needed: if your work could inadvertently inflict an injury or loss on the clients—such as tax preparation. Estimated cost of average coverage: comes with small-business insurance; minimum premium approximately $500.

Partnership Insurance

Partnership insurance protects you against suits arising from the actions of any partners in the business. When needed: if you have partners or do joint ventures. Estimated cost of average coverage: a $500 fidelity bond.

Small-Business Insurance

This provides coverage for business losses—including general liability, business interruption, and loss of earnings, errors and omissions, and product liability. These policies can be purchased separately as well. When needed: if you have more extensive inventory or equipment than you can protect by adding a business endorsement or rider to the homeowner's policy. Estimated cost of average coverage: $500 per year.

Workers Compensation Insurance

If you have people working for you (employees), you need to provide them with Workers Compensation Insurance. The cost of this insurance will be based on the business classification and total payroll.

This compensates employees for costs of work-related injuries and also time off the job. When needed: available primarily for employees. If you are incorporated you can get this insurance for yourself. State regulations vary. May be called state disability insurance. Estimate cost of average coverage: bare bones coverage, about $200 per year.

Contact a company called State Fund (www.scif.com) in California for coverage. In Arizona contact SCF Arizona at 602-631-2600 or 800-231-4453 www.SCFAZ.com.

In Nevada, every business that employs anyone must obtain workers compensation insurance coverage unless that entity is certified by the Commissioner of Insurance as a self-insured employer. Contact the State of Nevada Department of Business and Industry Division of Insurance 702-486-4009 2501 E Sahara Ave Ste 302, Las Vegas NV 89158.

Bonded

Being bonded means that an outside agency (the bonding company) is making a guarantee. For instance, if you were a home cleaning service the bond would mean individuals are not felons and nothing will get stolen.

Grand theft is a crime recognized as a felony by most US States, and involves the deprivation of property. The dollar value could be as low as $400. Check your states for what they consider grand theft.

For more information on bonding, search the Internet for Getting Bonded for Small Business and you will find companies that provide this service.

The SBA can be a great source for some of your insurance questions. Call Termquote (800-444-8376) for more information and education. Additional resources: www.4Insurance.com (life, health, auto and home); www.MatrixDirect.com (key person insurance); www.InsureMe.com; www.INSWeb.com (renters, business). Check out these Web sites as they have information and knowledge that may be of benefit to you: www.quotesmith.com; www.e-insure.com; www.insweb.com; www.bestquote.com; and www.quickquote.com.

There are other things that you need to deal with as a business. They're not difficult but at times are confusing. The city or state may require a business license. If you're dealing with food, it's the health department. Then there's sales tax for the state. Guarantees, warranties and other stuff will be uncomplicated here.

From time to time, you may need an attorney to guide you through the many and varying aspects of your business. We used a prepaid legal service, which costs approximately $35 per month. This gives you access to an attorney when you need it without breaking the bank. This is a great solution for the start-up, home-based, mail order and Internet business. One of their services is that they will review contracts. Prepaid Legal Svcs Inc provides this service. Go to our Web site (www.RoundsMiller.com), click on the link to find out more about this search. We have used it for years.

City Business License

If your business is going to operate within the law, it may be necessary to obtain a license or permit in the city or county in which you will be doing business. If the business is a service and performs any portion of its work in cities outside its operational center, you may be required to obtain licenses in those cities as well. For a start-up, home-based, mail order or Internet business, the location of your office may determine your city for a city license, not where your clients are located. Different cities have different requirements for the business license.

There have been some interesting stories about cities enforcing the business license. One city's employees would go to weddings and when the photographer took the first picture inquired to the photographer whether they had a city business license.

A student shared that he was unloading into the client's living room from his truck which was parked in the driveway of the client's home. As he turned around, there was a police officer asking about the city's business license.

Another city requires that you have to park the car in the garage (you can't change the garage into a recording studio and then park the car on the street). Several cities require that you notify the neighbors. Some cities have the fire inspector look over the business.

Different types of businesses may be subject to special restrictions (or zoning). For instance, a mail order business may be allowed in the home while a direct-sales operation may not. Repair services may be allowed only if they don't involve the use of toxic chemicals. Food services may be disallowed. The city may allow the home as an administrative office for the business.

Home-based businesses are not permitted to change the appearance of the neighborhood. A home-based business may be prohibited from using advertising or equipment that can be viewed from the street. Some cities restrict all home-based business operation.

Business licenses provide the city with a source of revenue and a means of controlling the types of businesses that operate within their jurisdictions. The way the cities computes that license is different. Our city has a base and then a couple of dollars for every $X over that. Other cities are based on the number of employees.

City business licenses are renewable yearly (January-December) or annually from when you first applied for the license. The cost is around $100+ per year.

The application will consist of such specifics as name, business address, type of business, number of employees, expected gross, vehicles to be operated, and any other information that may be relevant.

In Nevada a business license (state business license) is needed for each person, corporation, partnership, business association and any other similar organization that conducts an activity for profit. Obtain the license from the Department of Taxation. Business License Office: 500 S Grand Central Pkwy, Las Vegas, NV 89101 702-455-4252. The local SBA may be able to assist you with the business license.

In the City of Los Angeles, a Business Tax Registration Certificate (TRC) is the original copy of your Business License and is about $99 a year. A small business with $100,000 or less of taxable and nontaxable gross receipts may qualify for a Small Business Exemption.

In Riverside the business license fees are $45 for initial licensing and $30 for annual renewal for unincorporated areas of Riverside County. Fee exemptions are granted for various agricultural activities, certain residential businesses, places of worship, and specific nonprofit organizations.

Nearly all cities require a city business license. Call your local city hall and ask for the city license desk. Ask what the guidelines are for a start-up, home-based, mail order or Internet business.

Car Sign

If you would like to use your automobile to advertise your business, check with your local city hall for guidelines. One city we checked with allowed home-based businesses to advertise on one vehicle only.

If you live in a homeowners association, a vehicle with signage may be considered a commercial vehicle. The homeowners association may have regulations for commercial vehicles—such as parking outside the complex rather than on the street or in guest parking.

If you have a sign on your car, you may be considered a commercial vehicle and subject to a commercial vehicle registration.

Nancy had a situation where a car sign would have made her client unhappy. Nancy went to the home of a client to help him organize and de-clutter his home, and he had a panic attack when he saw her car in his driveway. What if the car had a huge neon sign on it saying CLUTTEROLOGIST? What would the neighbor's think!

Sales Tax Permit

If you are selling a product, you need to collect sales tax. If you are going to a store, purchasing products for your clients and then asking the client to reimburse you, then you will not be dealing with sales tax.

These may be called a resale number, a wholesale number or a tax exempt number, and all of these deal with the sales tax. In the State of California this is called the Seller's Permit.

If you are providing a service, installation or repairs, you do not have to have a sales tax permit.

If you fabricate or assemble the product, you add sales tax and you would need a sales tax permit. You have made the product more valuable by putting it together.

Anyone who purchases items for resale or who provides a taxable service must obtain a seller's permit number.

You can easily apply for a permit by calling the State Board of Equalization, going to their office, or using their Web site.

Many states have temporary seller's permits. For instance, if you sell Christmas trees, your business isn't for the full year, just November and December. If you are exhibiting at a tradeshow, conference, or convention, talk to the coordinator as they may issue you a run-of-the-show seller's permit.

Identifying Sale Tax

So, how do you let the clients know about sales tax? There are three ways that you can list (identify) sales tax for your clients:

Post a sign stating that sales tax will be added (like at McDonalds).

List a separate amount for sales tax ($19.95 plus $1.40 sales tax).

Specifically include sales tax ($30 including sales tax), like prices listed at a swap meet or street fair.

What rate do you charge for clients in other states? You only charge clients in your state, because that's where your business is. Have you seen an ad, like Lillian Vernon states: shipments to NV, NY State, SC, TN, VA and VT, apply the applicable sales tax. They are collecting sales tax in those states because they have a base of operation in those states. There is no such thing as a multiple-state sale tax. A company such as Starbucks would collect sales tax in all 50 states because they have stores in all 50 states.

There is no such thing as an Internet tax where purchases on the Internet are taxed. If you do make a purchase on the Internet and the business' physical presences is in your state, then the business would charge the appropriate state sales tax rate.

As of this time, the State of New York has created what is called an Amazon tax which could be tax/sales tax for online purchases. With the change in the economy, everyone is looking for a new source of income. Time will tell if an Amazon tax happens or not.

If you don't have a seller's permit and a client pays you sales tax, you must turn the sales tax over to the state (or return in back to the client). If the client overpays you sales tax, you must either return the excess to the client or turn the excess over to the state.

IRS

This is the exciting part about being a business. There are more business expenses that are deductable when you are a business than when you are an individual. Whether you are a sole proprietorship, partnership or LLC, it's all the same to the IRS (for our discussion here).

If you or your spouse has a full-time job (we'll call you W2'd [Wage and Tax Statement]) when you become a business, you might be able to bring home more money on your W2'd pay check. Here's the scoop.

When you filled out the withholding form for your W4 (Employee's Withholding Allowance Certificate), the number of deduction/withholdings may be small (one or two, for instance). When you create the business, the business will have business expenses (Schedule C on your income taxes). You can change the number of withholdings to a larger number for instance (check with your accountant).

However (and this is the good part) your W2'd pay check is regular income. So these expenses are balanced against the W2'd income. You can wait until next year when you get your refund. Or you can revise your withholdings to a larger number of deductibles. Check with your accountant to determine which would be best in your situation.

Open For Business

With a home-based business, you open your doors for business and then buy the things you need. Those expenses (most of them) are a business expense in the current year. Isn't that great! Today I am a business. Tomorrow I create business expenses.

Let's say that we wanted to open a beauty salon. The first thing we would do is find a place to rent, and they would want a deposit, first month and last month's rent. Then you have to buy the equipment: chairs, mirrors and shampoo. The sign outside the building doesn't come for free. The utilities have to be hooked up. And an ad in the newspaper and radio to announce your grand opening are additional expenses. Now the doors are open for business.

Every expense that happened before the doors opened for business has to be amortized (gradual and periodic reduction of the amount) over a period of time (seven years for instance). So it would be years before you got to enjoy the benefit of those expenses. Let's hope that you're still in business.

Many people ponder the difference between what is a hobby and a business. Here are three factors:

First, in order to take business expenses, you must have a legitimate business. If you create a business just to be able to take advantage of all the home-based business expenses, it is not considered a legitimate business.

Second, prove that you intend to make a profit. A good way to accomplish this is to create a business plan. Attend a seminar given by the Small Business Administration on creating a business plan. There is a difference between intending to make a profit and actually making a profit. There will be times in the life of your business when you have more expenses than income. That's part of business.

Third, work your business on a regular and consistent base. For instance, if you have a multilevel business and are working 40 hours a week for a company, in your calendar enter that for 60 minutes at a time four or five times a week that you are in the office working on the multilevel business.

Document your income and expenses. Just because this may be a part-time business for you doesn't mean you can keep any less documentation than a full-time business.

With a home-based business, your intent is to make a profit and work the business actively and consistently. There are types of businesses that even if there is no profit, won't be considered a hobby. The American auto industry is not a hobby and doesn't often make a profit!

Being a poor business person or not having a business that your family approves of, doesn't make it a hobby.

Accounting Software

From the simplest two-column ledger program like Quicken to the completely integrated multitasking, relational accounting programs like Peachtree, accounting software is one of the best reasons to be computerized. Find a program that is appropriate for your needs, style, and business. Talk to your accountant about what software can be imported into his or her system.

If your rule for business is that EVERYTHING goes through the checkbook (you don't pay with cash, you deposit the cash you receive), then having a simple program like Quicken will probably work just fine.

A couple of years ago, Nancy took a class at the local adult school for QuickBooks. What she learned was that some of her questions were not about the software at all. They were accounting questions. So, she took another class on accounting. Basic understanding helps you to be able to ask the questions of your accountant and to use their terms and language. If you are not familiar with accounting procedures, we recommend you take a class or get a good book on the subject.

Here are some common business expenses.

- Mortgage interest or rent
- Gas, electric, water and sewer
- Cleaning crews to dust, vacuum, and empty the trash

- Computers, copiers, fax machines and telephones
- Paper, pens, ink cartridges, postage and postage stamps
- Desks, sofas, coffee tables and other furniture
- Painting, wallpaper, carpeting, and other repairs or remodeling
- Phone bills, cell phones, pagers, and Personal Data Assistants (PDA's)
- Newspapers, magazines, books, and online media subscriptions
- Plane fares, hotel, meal, and rental car
- Health, life, dental, vision, disability, and unemployment insurance premiums
- Contributions to Employee Retirement Plans
- Company cars, and even boats
- Advertising
- Bank charges and banking fees
- Charitable contributions
- Credit card fees
- Permits and licenses
- Repairs
- Other expenses that qualifies as ordinary and necessary to operate the business

Documentation

As a business, you should be keeping two pieces of documentation to backup your business tax expenses.

The first is the cancelled check or bank or credit card statement. Let's say that you go to Office Depot and purchase $100 worth of office supplies. You mutter under your breath, "Why can't the IRS just take my check as the documentation."

That's because the store may ask, "Would you like cash back?" Your eyes light up and you ask for $100.

The second piece of documentation is the receipt, invoice or statements showing exactly what you purchased and for how much. Now your check is $200, of which only $100 is office supplies. Or you buy $50 worth of office supplies and $50 worth of candy. This process is called itemization (to list) by the IRS.

If you don't use a check for purchases, a credit card is fine. A credit card has a monthly statement. That statement cannot be altered which is what the IRS is looking for. The NCR copy of your check could be altered as can data in accounting software.

A good policy is to keep documentation for all transactions. Don't assume that if a transaction is under a low dollar figure that the IRS would never ask for it.

One of the most important pieces of documentation is your calendar. Our advice to you is to keep the calendar forever. And the messier (more used) it is, the better.

For instance, let's say the IRS questions a business meal that you had. You pull out your calendar and say "see here it shows that I meet Joe at Cheesecake" which was exactly the same thing your receipt indicated.

The IRS doesn't care if you eat at El Cheapo or Chez Expensive for a business expense. A business expense is a business expense. As the business owner, know the difference between cash flow and an IRS expense. With cash flow, you have to have the money in your checkbook to pay for it. So although the IRS doesn't care, the banks don't like you having overdrafts.

Just because you could buy a very expensive car for the business doesn't mean that you should. An expensive car as a business expense doesn't make it cheaper, less expensive or better for you. If you don't have the cash flow to support the car in the first place, taking the business expense in the second place may cause problems.

Intentions

One of the easiest ways to think about whether an expense is a personal or a business expense is to think about the intention of that expense.

For instance if you and another person (not someone working in your business) go out for a meal and you want to pick up the check as a business expense there needs to be a discussion about business. On the receipt jot a note about what was discussed, who you were with, where the meal was, when it was (the date), and how much was spent.

Do you want to go to Hawaii and call that a business trip? It could be, if done correctly. Before you go to Hawaii, you have to set up business meetings. The meetings should be during the whole time you are there. It doesn't have to be every day and every hour, but it can't be just the first day.

If you have gone to Hawaii and while you were sitting at the beach, you started a conversation with the stranger next to you. He likes you and later becomes your best client. Is that trip a business expense? No. You didn't go to Hawaii with the intention of creating business, it just happened. You didn't set up the meeting on the beach as a business meeting, it just happened.

Sharing Equipment

When you start your business, you may want to use what you already own because cash flow is tight.

For those items that you have one of (one car, one computer, or one telephone), then you have to log the use of personal and business.

Car: go to the office supply store and get an auto mileage book. Every time you drive the car, write down the mileage and purpose (personal or business). At the end of the month, add up your business mileage.

Computer: document the usage of the computer for the business. At the end of the month, add it up. This will give you the base price for your Internet service. If you use the computer 20 percent for business, then 20 percent of the provider's bill is a business expense.

Telephone: if you have one phone line, then you must document the business use of that phone. The base charges for the phone are expensed to your personal use. The actual business use is a business expense. When the bills arrive, get out your highlighter and highlight the calls that were business. Add up the cost.

Not Sharing Equipment

When you have more than one item or an item that is used exclusively for business and is in the business name, this is how you document the item for your financial records.

Car: if you have two vehicles, decide which one is for business and which one is for personal. All of the expenses for the business vehicle are a business expense.

There are two methods of calculating the expenses of a vehicle. If you don't want to keep all your receipts, you can average the cost by using the government's mileage of 58.5¢ per mile. You may be surprised to know that you are not making money or even breaking even with this method. Most vehicles cost more than 58.5¢ to operate. The advantage is less paperwork.

The other method is actual expense. Keep your gasoline receipts, your insurance costs, your vehicle maintenance and even your vehicle payments.

Computer: If you were to be visited by the IRS and only had one computer, it might be difficult to convince them that you have no personal life and don't use the computer for personal use. Have your kids put games on the computer? The only games that can be on your business computer are those that came with it (like Microsoft solitaire). If there are games, the line to personal usage has been crossed.

Holiday Cards: your holidays cards might be considered a business expense if they promote the business. For instance just signing the holiday cards Mike and Nancy would be considered a personal expense.

On the other hand having the cards pre-printed:

Rounds, Miller and Associates
Mike Rounds and Nancy Miller

could be considered a business expense.

Business Meals
When you go out to eat, keep the receipts. On the recipe document the date, the amount, who you had a meeting with, and what business was discussed. A common misunderstanding is that you don't have to talk the whole time about business. You DO have to talk about business.

If you are a sales person (or making a sales call) also indicate what the percentage of likihood is that this person/company will become a client. What the IRS is looking for, if you're taking all your cousins out the dinner, one at a time, and calling it a sales call. None of your cousins ever intended to become a client.

Why are business travel meals only a 50 percent business expense? Because the IRS doesn't reward you for eating. You have to eat anyway. The difference between the business travel meal and the business meal is in the documentation. A business travel meal does not need to contain talking about business to be expense.

A word of advice about locations of meeting for meals. There must be a reasonable expectation of a conversation. A night club, although they may have great food would not necessarily be a reasonable expectation for a conversation with the hundreds of people dancing and talking with the music blaring in the background.

Home-Office Deduction
To calculate how much of the rent, mortgage interest, and other home expenses can reasonably be deducted, measure the floor space of the home office and divide it by the total area of your house. If your office space comes to 9.5 percent, you can deduct 9.5 percent of the cost of the rent, insurance, mortgage interest, utilities, repairs, and improvements to the property.

The drawback to these prorated deductions is that, since part of the house will be considered business property, the business will be subject to capital gains tax when the house is sold. However, a while ago, the dollar figure has been raised where this is now an almost non-issue.

To qualify to claim expenses for business use of your home, you must meet the following tests.

Your use of the business part of your home must be:

1. Exclusive use. You must use your home business area only for your business. You do not meet the requirements of the exclusive use test if you use the area in question both in business and for personal purposes.

2. Regular. You must use a specific area of your home for business on a continuing basis. For instance 45-60 minutes a day, 4-5 days a week (12 hours a month).

3. For your business. You have no other location where you conduct substantial administrative or management activities of your business.

AND . . . the business part of your home must be **one** of the following

1. Your principal place of business, or

2. You regularly and exclusively use your home office for administrative or management activities for your business and have no other fixed location where you perform such activities, or

3. A place where you meet or deal with clients in the normal course of your business,

   or

4. You run a day care center at home, or

5. A separate structure (not attached to your home) you use in connection with your business.

Let's take a closer look at exclusive use. That means that your office is your office. Not a place where guests sometimes sleep. Not a place where you store extra clothes in the closet. Look at the bookshelf in the office. What are the titles of the books? Nancy's bookshelf has books like *Taming the Paper Tiger*, Time Management for Dummies and Sidetracked Home Executives. Although you may think these are personal books, as a Professional Organizer, Nancy reads books on organizing and therefore these are business books and are allowable on the bookshelf in the office.

I haven't talked about business entertainment and we're not going to. This is an area that is abused so if you have business entertainment issues, research how to document your activities.

There is a book that is only available through the Internet. Home Business Tax Savings Made Easy! (formerly It's How Much You Keep that Counts) that gives tax tips to learn how to keep more of your money.

A great book to answer almost all your questions about what and how to take home-business expenses (as well as other books) is the book Home Business Tax Deductions for $34.99. The publisher (Nolo Press www.Nolo.com) is a wonderful resource for home-based businesses. Nolo Press was created by a group of lawyers, and their books deal with a range of legal type issues written in an easy to understand and comprehend fashion.

Two free IRS publications explain the rules for home offices and offer advice on bookkeeping: Business Use of Your Home #587, and Taxpayers Starting a Business #583. Call 800-829-3676. Deliveries of these publications are within 7-15 working days of request. Or you can go online and get a PDF of these publications.

Credit Cards

Your ability to accept your client's credit card is called a Merchant Account. The quickest and cheapest way to do this is through PayPal.

There is no setup or monthly fees with PayPal. The discount fee is 1.9 to 2.9 percent + 30¢ per transaction. They accept international payments from 37 countries. You have to wait three to four business days for the funds to be transferred to your merchant bank account. Our experience has been that the funds are transferred faster than three days.

PayPal has a **face to face** (merchant) account. With this account, you put the MasterCard, Visa and American Express logos on your Web site. You process the credit card, rather than going thru PayPal. The fee is $30 per month.

If you already have a consumer PayPal account and now apply for a merchant account, because your social security number is the same, it will take an extra day for PayPal to get the authorization from you that you to make sure that you are the same person (consumer and vendor) and not using a stolen social security number or have incorrectly inputted the wrong number.

For the customer, the name recognition is invaluable. Almost everyone has heard of PayPal especially if they have purchased something with eBay. If the customer doesn't want to give you their credit card number, they don't have to. This is secured information with PayPal.

For the merchant, there is no application fee, no monthly minimums, no additional software or hardware to purchase, and no statement fee.

You can TALK to a person. After you sign-in to your account, at the bottom, click on Contact Us, on the right side look for Contact Us by phone or e-email (click on that). Then click on Call us. There will be a PIN number and PayPal's 800 number. You call the 800 number and enter your PIN number and that gives you access to a LIVE PERSON!

Another easy place to establish your merchant status is with your **Costco** Executive or Sam's Club Business membership. Your membership must be at their highest level, then go to the customer service counter and ask for a merchant status application. They have twisted the arm of a merchant bank to provide a very good rate for their members. However, as long as you use that merchant bank, you must maintain your club membership.

The total time it should take you to get established with a merchant account is from three weeks to three months. Give yourself enough time to get all the paperwork in and the processing done. It can be done more quickly.

Now that you know about the organizing business, the steps to set up the business, you need clients—marketing. Here are some low-cost and no-cost to get clients in the next chapter.

Getting the BUSINESS

Section 3: Getting the Business

No matter what business you start. It is important to advertise. Without clients, even the best business in the world will fail. Here are low-cost and no-cost ways for you to develop your business. Some methods are time intensive while costing little money. Some will work for you, others may not. Welcome to Business.

What are you? A consultant, a trainer, a coach or a house cleaner? What you call yourself may determine not only what you are expected to do but whether or not you'll be hired at all. Because of the colloquial interpretations of words and titles, different names have come to denote different expectations on the part of the client.

1. A consultant, by definition defines the problem and then does the work for the client. For example, if you are a graphic design consultant, the client will expect you to actually create the finished designs for them.

2. A trainer transfers knowledge to the client, their staff, or their employees and bears no responsibility for its application or usage. A personal physical trainer at the gym is an example. The trainer is transferring (telling or lecturing) to the client. Think of a personal trainer at the gym. The person is there suggesting a workout schedule, helping you, encouraging you. You have to do the work!

3. A coach imparts or transfers knowledge and/or processes and then works with the client to apply what was transferred. A person who teaches time management and then works with attendee on time management goals that are developed by the client. I have become a Certified Professional Coach so that I could specifically add telephone coaching to help clients.

4. Hands-on organizing. Working with the client, side-by-side, digging in and actually clearing out, and doing the work. Setting up systems, hauling away donations, taking out trash, providing encouragement.

If you find that there is some level of overlap between the information—you'll probably be applying all of the elements at one time or another in your career even though you label yourself as one of the primary titles shown above.

Free or Fee

One of the most common questions asked is: Should the first meeting with a potential client be free or fee?

The most powerful form of convincing a client to purchase is called sample selling. Few of us would purchase a vehicle without a test drive or a sampling of the features and performance. One of the best techniques for getting prospects to come and see us is to offer the first session for free. This gets the parties interested.

Offering to assist a prospect on a no-charge basis is an excellent way to introduce your skills and services to the prospects. Unfortunately, as a Professional Organizer, once you give away some of your services, many people begin to believe that the services are worth what they pay for them—nothing.

Rather than opening yourself up to a flood of no profit consultations, ask for a nominal donation (for example $20) for a favorite charity.

This simple device benefits everyone because:

1. You get the prospect to pay you a visit so you can explore the possibility of working together.

2. By requesting a tax-deductible donation, you stop people who aren't serious from coming and wasting your time.

3. The charity benefits each time a visit is made.

Regardless of what arrangements you make with a client, it is in your best interest to spend about ten minutes of the first meeting obtaining the answers to these five questions:

1. What are the client's goals and objectives? Don't guess at the prospect's needs no matter how astute you are. Let the prospect tell you what they're looking for. Later on, you can add your assessment of their needs to the conversation or proposal.

2. What are the impediments to the client's achieving these goals? Let the prospect tell you what they think needs to be done to correct the deficiencies. Even if it's incorrect, it'll give them a greater feeling of importance if they believe that they've got the problems figured out and are hiring a organizer because it's easier than doing it themselves.

3. How does the client feel about change? Professional organizers have been known to cause more change per hour than any employee. If a prospect has an attitude of fix it but don't change it, you can be assured that consulting services are being considered as an excuse for internal problems that they feel cannot be corrected and all they want is someone to blame.

4. If the client could have three wishes granted for success, what would they be? Let the prospect tell you what their goals and ambitions are. Once you know what they expect to accomplish, it becomes much easier for you to develop a proposal that fits their defined needs rather than your assessment of their needs.

5. Have you ever used a Professional Organizer before?

In one of my clutter classes, a student shared that she had hired a Professional Organizer. The organizer rate was $90 per hour and her assistant was $45 per hour. The first thing the organizer did was to go shopping for expensive organizing containers. The organizer never did organize anything. The woman who shared this experience now believes that all organizers charge the same way!

If a prospect has never used a Professional Organizer before, they may tend to treat you as an employee. If this is the case, you will have to educate them on how to correctly and effectively work with them. This is a question that you will have to assess because if you aren't interested in schooling these individuals, you may not want to have them as clients.

Establishing Your Fee

Services must be correctly and fairly priced, or you'll never be profitable. Below is a simplified method to help you profitably price your services. The average Professional Organizer fee is between $35 and $200 per hour. Corporate rates are slightly higher. Most Organizers charge by the hour, some by the project or type of service.

Daily Labor Rate

The Daily Labor Rate is your worth as a labor commodity. To accurately define this worth, you can look up your labor classification by geographic locale in the Wage and Salary Almanac at the library's reference section or visit www.salary.com.

This is an example of how to calculate your worth as a labor commodity:

1. $75,000 per year (a nominal figure in today's labor market) (12 months or 260 days).

2. A consultant works approximately 64 percent (168 days) of the time for the same amount of money.

3. $75,000 √ 168 = $446 per day or $56 per hour.

4. Overhead is approximately 90 percent.

5. Profit is approximately 10 percent.

Calculating Daily Billing Rate		
Daily Labor Rate		$446
Overhead	90 percent of daily labor rate	$401
Profit	10 percent of daily labor rate + 10 percent of overhead	$ 85
Daily Billing Rate		$932 per day or $117 per hour

People who provide services generate two types of expenses.

1. Overhead is the cost of being in business, and includes general operating expenses plus all other expenses that are incurred, regardless of how many clients there are or how much business you are doing. Rent is an example of overhead.

2. Direct expenses are those incurred for a particular client or a particular client's project. They are called direct because the client is charged for expenses directly. For example, the cost to fly to a meeting for the client is billed to the client.

Overhead is calculated on an annual basis and is a simple equation. It is the estimated total annual expenses for the business divided by the estimated total annual revenues for the business.

The anticipated cost of running the business is $67,500 and the revenues generated to be $75,000.

Category of Expense	Monthly	Annual
Part-time secretary	$1,000	$12,000
Office rent	1,000	12,000
Telephone and postage	550	6,600
Automotive	300	3,600
Personnel benefits/employment taxes	600	7,200
Equipment and supplies	300	3,600
Marketing costs	1,000	12,000
Dues and subscriptions	100	1,200
Business licenses and taxes	75	900
Insurance	300	3,600
Accounting and legal	200	2,400
Miscellaneous	200	2,400
Total	$5,625	$67,500

The equation is then: $67,500 √ $75,000 = 90 percent

Profit is whatever is left after you have paid yourself (salary) and paid for the operating expenses of the business.

We have assigned a nominal 10 percent profit to the equation. You can use any number that makes sense to you. Of all the elements, this is the one with the most flexibility because making a profit is not essential for the business to operate. It may be essential for future growth, but based on pure mathematics, it is not necessary for the project under consideration to be successful.

Don't ignore profit. You're entitled to make a profit just like anybody else, but it's the first place you start to cut and make concessions in a proposal without affecting the payoff and actual operating expenses.

When calculating profit, take the percentage from the sum of the overhead and the daily labor rate. The overhead is money that is NOT earning interest in the bank, so it's acceptable to make a profit on the money you're using to run the business to compensate for the interest you are not earning on it.

Another way is to calculate what you want to earn per year.
How many hours a month do you want to work? 16 hours a month (just the one weekend a month)?

$25 x 16 hours per month x 12 months = $4800
$35 x 16 hours per month x 12 months = $6720

If you double your hours (32 hours per month) the number would look like:

$25 x 32 hours per month x 12 months = $6720
$35 x 32 hours per month x 12 months = $13440

Value Considerations

Regardless of your financial calculations, many factors affect the actual fees that organizing charge. Some of the common factors are as follows:

1. Reputation affects the fee a Professional Organizer can command and may be based on how noted you are in the field. The more distinguished, the more that can be charged. Fees are a function of value, and value is a function of reputation in the eyes of prospects.

2. Prevailing Rate is sometimes a daily or hourly standard rate dictated by tradition within a given field or in a given area of the country.

3. Value Added Fees are based on the results that the expects to achieve and their worth to the client in real dollars. The organizer's track record and reputation play heavily in this approach.

Don't be afraid or ashamed to work at a reduced fee or at a prevailing rate. Many organizers who have inflexible policies about their rates go bankrupt waiting to be paid what they think they're worth. Dollars are dollars and if you make yours a nickel at a time, that's OK—they still pay the bills.

The simplest philosophy is this: "When your calendar is filled with full fee assignments, you cannot afford to work for a reduced fee. Until that day, don't turn down any assignment that pays you for your efforts."

Credibility

When you buy a product, you can see it, feel it, smell it, touch it, or taste it. When you offer services, the prospect prefers to experience us and to build trust and eliminate their doubts about hiring us. This is called establishing credibility.

The hierarchy for establishing your credibility as service providers is as follows:

1. Personal experience—when clients have first-hand experience with your skills they have the inherent knowledge of what your capabilities are and whether you are a fit for their needs.

2. Recommendation from a trusted peer—prospects have defined job responsibilities that parallel those of others. A solid recommendation from one of these peers who have experienced your skills is a great way to get an opportunity to offer your services.

3. Recommendations from a prospect's vendor—many prospects will ask for referrals from vendors that are doing good work for them and whose opinion they value.

4. Promotional materials generated by the organizer—you can put anything into your promotional materials that you think will attract and impress the prospect. Unfortunately, most prospects are skeptical of promotional materials and prefer some form of experience, either directly or by referral, as to your capability to handle their requirements.

Establishing your credibility with your prospect is an integral part of being hired because people see what they believe and when they believe that you are credible, they tend to trust and subsequently hire you.

Contracts

To ensure that all parties in an arrangement understand everything that is involved, a written agreement is a necessity. These agreements are not intended for litigation purposes as much as they are for the purpose of clarification and understanding.

Aside from the obvious legal protection with a contract, it has many other advantages. One of the important advantages of a contract is that it demonstrates to the client that you take your own business responsibilities seriously and professionally.

Here's a special tip that has been gained through years of experience: If you quote a fee on a fixed-price or fixed-fee basis, quote an odd number. If your calculation shows that the total cost of doing the client's assignment is $10,511, resist the tendency to round the quotation to $10,500. Doing so gives the appearance that you rounded up, not down.

Several styles of contracts are included here as a foundation for your business and we encourage you to use them, in any form you find expedient, as often as possible to ensure that all the parties involved get what they want and need out of the organizing arrangement. Use these agreements as the basic form for your needs, and then take the completed filled-in form(s) to legal counsel. Counsel then can watch for specifics, which apply to the situation. Generally, it costs less to review a document than to create it.

The contracts and agreements most commonly used by organizers are:

- Letter of Agreement
- Formal Contract or Legalese Style

The actual proposal that is prepared and submitted may be of different formats and lengths. Any agreement is only as valid as the integrity of the persons who are involved.

Letter of Agreement

The Letter of Agreement can be informal or formal. With some clients, informal is better. Be sure to break down the essence and particulars of the agreement. This letter causes both of you to recall more clearly and behave more predictably.

This would not have be a letter, it could be an e-mail if you would like. Keeping it informal.

Sample Letter of Agreement

February 30, 2025

John Smith
Home Appliance Repair Service
1234 Central
Los Angeles, CA 98765

Dear John:

Thanks for the opportunity to be of service to you and your firm. With all the changes in business processes that have occurred, it's only natural for paper and file handling processes to require an overhaul.

We propose to do a combination of analysis and redesign wherever the system needs a fresh approach to maintain your organization's efficiency.

What we propose to do is as follows:

- Analyze your current systems for handling paper mail, filing, and routing it, and design a more effect method for your current business operations. This will include reducing the actual volume of paper mail received sent, and filed.

- We will document, the processes, implement them, and train your personnel in the effective use and maintenance of the systems.

The processes, as described, should take approximately three days and the delivery, implementation and training will occur simultaneously.

The cost for the services as described is $3,200 and our terms for this program are as follows:

A deposit of $1,600 is to accompany a signed copy of this letter contract.

All materials and labor will be itemized. When each of the tasks as outlined above is completed, we will invoice you for the amount due. The first $1,600 will be credited back to you, and the balance will be due and payable net seven days.

If you have any questions or require any additional information, please feel free to call on us.

Sincerely

Joanna Doe

Joanna Doe

I agree with and approve the letter contract outlined above and want to proceed with the program as proposed.

____________________________ ________________

John Smith Date

Formal Contract or Legalese Style

Many people who have transitioned from large corporations and the military or aerospace industries prefer these because they include contingency provisions for just about anything that might go wrong. This is a more comprehensive type of agreement, which actually incorporates a organizing contract, statement of work, confidentiality agreement, terms, conditions, and timeline all in a single document.

The caution in using these lengthy and complicated agreements is that if you are not comfortable with them or do not understand the exact meaning of the terminology used, seek the assistance of someone who does.

These contracts are not intended as an instrument to cheat you. If you inadvertently sign and agree to something that you do not understand, you may be committing yourself to performance that is either not what you intended, or that is outside your scope of capability to provide.

Sample Formal Contract

Consulting Agreement Between

Joanna Doe, Professional Organizer
Your Company Name
6138 Ridgepath Court
Rancho Palos Verdes CA 90275-3248
310-544-9502
www.YourWebSite.com

and

Byte Size Computer School
11460 Warm St
Central Valley, CA 92777
(800) 555-2093

SERVICES: Joanna Doe will perform the services to develop a legal filing system which includes recommended hardware and software to assist in the organization, filing, and maintenance of Byte Size's contracts, agreements, proposals, and invoicing systems.

TASK 1: Analyze the current system for inputting, recording, routing, filing, and retrieving client inquiries, proposals, contracts, and invoices.

TASK 2: Design a system that works efficiently within the current constraints and operating rules of both the business and the legal requirements for retention, maintenance, and storage of records.

TASK 3: Research and recommend software systems and training that will help streamline the systems as defined in items #1 and #2 above.

COMPENSATION: As full compensation for the services to be performed by Joanna Doe, Byte Size shall pay Joanna Doe per the terms and agreement as outlined below:

- The sum of $2,000 shall be paid to Joanna Doe at the onset of work, which is to be coincidental with the signing of this agreement.

- The sum of $3,000 shall be paid to Joanna Doe upon completion of the three tasks as outlined above.

In support of this effort, it is mutually understood, and agreed to by both Joanna Doe and Byte Size, that Byte Size will supply to Joanna Doe full and complete description of all goods, services, contracts, and/or related items that are to be included and/or incorporated into the services as proposed. If requested and required, at the completion of the project, Joanna Doe shall surrender any and all documents and/or articles loaned to him by Byte Size in support of this project.

DELIVERY OF ITEMS/COMPLETION OF TASKS: All task items, #1 through #3, as delineated herein, shall, to the greatest extent practicable, be completed and accomplished to the satisfaction of Byte Size within 30 calendar days of the signing and acceptance of this agreement.

TRAVEL EXPENSES: Reasonable, out-of-pocket travel expenses (tourist-class transportation, hotel, and meals) incurred by Joanna Doe in connection with any trip made by Joanna Doe at the request and with prior approval of Byte Size will be paid by Byte Size.

INCIDENTAL EXPENSES: All mutually agreed upon expenses, which are either initialed or agreed upon in writing, actually incurred by Joanna Doe, incidental to the services performed, will be paid by Byte Size.

INVOICE AND PAYMENT: Joanna Doe shall submit invoices for services and expenses incurred (including receipts for items in excess of $25) and Byte Size shall make payment within seven days of the date of the invoice.

CONFIDENTIAL INFORMATION: Joanna Doe agrees not to disclose or to induce Byte Size to use any confidential information that may be acquired from any third-party during the term of this agreement. Joanna Doe represents that she is free to disclose to Byte Size, without breach of any obligation to a third-party, any and all information needed to perform services under this agreement. Joanna Doe further agrees to indemnify and hold Byte Size harmless from and against all losses, liabilities, damages, expenses, or claims against Byte Size based on a breach of obligation by Joanna Doe to a third-party in disclosing any third-party property to Byte Size during performance of the services under this agreement. During the course of performing services, Joanna Doe may become aware of and receive confidential information, including data, designs, ideas, methods, reports, plans, or other proprietary matters of Byte Size. Joanna Doe agrees to receive and hold in strict confidence for and on behalf of Byte Size all information that Joanna Doe creates in connection with or as a result of performing services under this agreement, including data, designs, ideas, methods, reports, suggestions, or other confidential information. Joanna Doe agrees not to use, or disclose, any of such information to any person either during or after the termination of this agreement unless such information is, or becomes, public knowledge.

INTELLECTUAL PROPERTY: All inventions, innovations, discoveries, improvements, ideas, and suggestions (rights), whether patentable or unpatentable, conceived, made, reduced to practice, or created by Joanna Doe, resulting from or arising out of the services performed by Joanna Doe under this agreement and relating in whole or in part to the business of Byte Size, will be promptly communicated in writing by Joanna Doe to Byte Size and shall become the sole property of Byte Size. Joanna Doe represents and warrants that Joanna Doe has no obligation to any third-party that would be breached by the disclosure and assignment of rights to Byte Size.

INDEPENDENT CONTRACTOR: Joanna Doe, with respect to the services performed under this agreement, is acting as an independent contractor, and not as an employee. Other persons, firms, or corporations during this agreement may employ Joanna Doe. Any employees or other personnel engaged by Joanna Doe shall be under the exclusive direction and control of Joanna Doe. Joanna Doe shall assume and discharge for her own account all costs, expenses, and charges necessary or incidental to the performance of services (mileage, telephone charges, etc).

TERM AND TERMINATION: This agreement is effective from the date first written below and shall terminate when the terms and conditions on the attached Statement of Work have been completed. This agreement may be terminated by Byte Size by giving three (3) days notice to Joanna Doe, in the event of death, illness or injury that will permanently prevent the performance of service required under this agreement, or if for any reason Joanna Doe fails to perform any services as delineated in this agreement, after request by Byte Size, for a period of four consecutive weeks. Either party may terminate this agreement on breach of any of the terms by the other party by giving three (3) days notice to the other party. In the event that Joanna Doe is in breach, and Byte Size cancels the contract, any advance monies shall be returned to Byte Size. In the event that Byte Size is in breach, and Joanna Doe cancels the contract, any and all monies paid to Joanna Doe shall remain the property of Joanna Doe and shall not be required to be returned. Termination of this agreement for any reason shall not affect Joanna Doe's obligation under paragraphs regarding Confidential Information and Intellectual Property and date is the date of receipt, since such date cannot be easily proved by the sender.

ENTIRE AGREEMENT: This agreement constitutes the entire agreement between the parties relating to the subject matter contained in it and supersedes all prior and contemporaneous representations, agreements, or understandings between the parties. No amendment or supplement of this agreement shall be binding unless executed in writing by the parties. No waiver of any one provision of this agreement shall constitute waiver of any other provision, nor shall any one waiver constitute a continuing waiver. In the event suit is brought to enforce or interpret any part of this agreement, the prevailing party shall be entitled to recover as an element of his costs of the suit, and not as damages, a reasonable attorney's fee to be fixed by the court. The "prevailing party" shall be the party who is entitled to recover the costs of suit, whether or not the suit proceeds to final judgment. A party not entitled to recover his costs shall not recover attorney's fees. No sum for attorney's fees shall be counted in calculating the amount of a judgment for purposes of determining whether a party is entitled to recover his costs or attorney's fees.

No waiver shall be binding unless executed in writing by the party against whom the waiver is asserted.

The terms, conditions, and statements contained herein are hereby mutually agreed upon as being the full and complete tasks required for the successful completion of this contract.

IN WITNESS WHEREOF, the parties hereto have signed on the day and year hereinafter set forth.

____

Joanna Doe Date

____

Byte Size Computer School Date

Confidentiality Agreement

When you go into a business or person's home, they are letting you have access to their deepest, darkest secrets. Although, you may care less about the contents of the documents, a Confidentiality Agreement should be signed to assure them that what you have access to, will be maintained in confidence.

Sample Confidentiality Agreement

Agreement/Acknowledgment between CLIENT and Professional Organizer.

Whereas, CLIENT agrees to furnish Professional Organizer certain confidential information relating to the affairs of CLIENT for purposes of review, revision, negotiation, and/or potential mutual business dealings, and

Whereas, Professional Organizer agrees to review, examine, inspect or obtain such information only for the purposes described above, and to otherwise hold such information confidential pursuant to the terms of this agreement,

BE IT KNOWN, that CLIENT has or shall furnish to Professional Organizer certain confidential information, and may further allow Professional Organizer the right to inspect the business of CLIENT and/or interview employees or representatives of CLIENT, all on the following conditions:

1. Professional Organizer agrees to hold all confidential or proprietary information or trade secrets ("information") in trust and confidence and agrees that it shall be used only for the contemplated purpose, and shall not be used for any other purpose or disclosed to any third party.

2. No copies will be made or retained of any written information supplied, other than for the specific and exclusive usage in conjunction with CLIENT.

3. At the conclusion of negotiations, or upon demand by CLIENT, all information, including written notes, photographs, memoranda, or notes taken by Professional Organizer may be requested to be returned to CLIENT.

4. This information shall not be disclosed to any employee or consultant unless they agree to execute and be bound by the terms of this agreement.

5. It is understood that Professional Organizer shall have no obligation with respect to any information known by Professional Organizer or generally known within the industry prior to date of this agreement, or which becomes common knowledge within the industry thereafter.

____________________________ __________________
Professional Organizer Date

____________________________ __________________
CLIENT Date

Photo and Video Release

If you would you would like to use pictures or video of work that you have done with a volunteer or client, you do need to get their permission. Written permission is best. Since most of your clients will be adults, this release is for an adult. If you will be working with a minor, find an appropriate minor's release.

Sample Photo and Video Release

I acknowledge that Professional Organizer is requesting permission to have my photographic and video images, as well as a photographic and video images of my property, which I testify that I own, if applicable, utilized by Professional Organizer.

I am granting Professional Organizer such permission, to use my photograph and video image and photographic and video images of my property, if applicable, in projects related to promoting my business and the professional organizing industry.

These images may include, but are not limited to, newsletters, references, written articles, promotional materials, and which maybe posted to my Web site, and/or other internet location, social media Web sites including, but not limited to, blogs, wiki's, social networking sites such as Facebook, LinkedIn, Twitter, Flickr, and YouTube.

I hereby give to Professional Organizer the right and permission to use my photographic and video image(s), and photographic and video image(s) of my property, if applicable. I agree that all photographic and video images of me and my property, if applicable, used and taken by Professional Organizer are owned by Professional Organizer and that Professional Organizer may copyright material containing same.

I agree not to authorize its use by anyone else. I waive any right to inspect or approve the finished copy, images, or printed matter that may be created in conjunction with this material.

I also agree that Professional Organizer shall be without liability to me for any distortion or illusionary effect resulting from the publication of my photographic images and/or video images and that nothing in this Release requires Professional Organizer to make any use of the rights it is acquiring.

I represent that this agreement does not in any way conflict with any other existing commitment on my part.

I have read the forgoing release agreement before affixing my signature below and certify that I fully understand the contents of this release.

Date: __________ Adult Signature: ____

Date: __________ Witness Signature: ____

Sub-Contractor Agreement

Occasionally, you may need additional help—workers. Instead of introducing these workers to your clients, you are coordinating the workers efforts on behalf of your clients. They are your sub-contractor. Here is a sample agreement.

Sample Sub-Contractor Agreement

This Sub-Contract Agreement (agreement) is made and effective this ____ day of ________ of 20____ by and between _____________ (sub-contactor) and Professional Organizer (our company).

1. The sub-contractor's relationship with our company is that of an independent entrepreneur providing organizing services to clients of our company.

2. The sub-contractor is not an employee of our company.

3. Our company will offer assignments on a sub-contract basis to sub-contractor as and when work volumes and project suitability permit. Our company makes no commitment as to the number of contracts for hours that will be offered.

4. Our company agrees to pay the sub-contractor at an agreed-upon rate of $_____ per hour for all organizing services provided by the sub-contractor at the request of our company. Our company will invoice the client directly for all services rendered and collect payment. The sub-contractor will invoice our company for their fees and payment will be made by our company to the sub-contractor on a bi-weekly basis.

5. The sub-contractor will be responsible for payment of any applicable taxes on all fees paid to the sub-contractor by our company.

6. The organizing services the sub-contractor will provide to clients will be those contracted for between the client and our company, and as described in the job description.

7. Our company will be responsible for business promotion and marketing of its services.

8. Our company will be responsible for client relationships except with respect to scheduling of appointments by the sub-contractor and client.

9. The sub-contractor will maintain the confidentiality of all client information, both business and personal.

10. The sub-contractor will maintain the confidentiality of all business information pertaining to our company and its operating.

11. The sub-contractor will respect the intellectual property right of our company. No documents, reports, presentations, processes or methodologies or systems of our company may be copied without the consent of our company.

12. Our company will provide appropriate training and support to the sub-contractor to enable them to perform all requested activities. Training and support will include regular follow-up sessions with the sub-contractor with regard to client activity.

13. Our company recommends that the sub-contractor arrange for appropriate business liability insurance with respect to actions taken by them on behalf of our company.

14. Both parties agree to review this agreement after a six-month period and to re-negotiate terms as required.

15. Either party with a minimum of two weeks' notice may terminate this agreement in regards to this particular client. The sub-contractor acknowledges that the client is a our company client and will not approach the client to perform services directly for them without the consent of our company.

______________________	______________________
Sub-Contractor	Professional Organizer Our Company
______________________	______________________
Date	Date

You are going to have to get the word out that you are in business and that is advertising. Some advertising is expensive and some advertising is inexpensive. However, the most inexpensive advertising that doesn't produce results is expensive. Track your results and modify your methods. Here are some low-cost, methods of advertising.

Postcards

Postcards are an often-overlooked method of using direct mail, both to build your own client list and to drive prospects to your Web site. First-class postage for postcards is 28¢ compared to 44¢ for an envelope.

Contact Modern Postcard (800-959-8365) www.ModernPostcard.com 250 four-color postcards printed for $95 [$19 for 25] or NoNEG Press (916-391-6797) http://business-card.com 1000 four-color postcards for $52. www.OverNightPrints.com prints 25 postcards for $3.93.

Do you think that postcards don't work or get read? In a survey by the USPS, they reported the following items were read immediately:

76.1 percent postcards
74.3 percent letter size envelope
71.8 percent larger than letter size envelope
70.5 percent newspaper or magazine
67.6 percent flyer
67.1 percent catalog

A minimum of three people will read a postcard. Postcards tend to be kept for a longer period of time, such as being posted on a bulletin board.

This custom cartoon was done by Brad Veley bveley@sbcglobal.net for a very reasonable price. It got me business!

On a direct mail envelope, the biggest issue is to get the envelope opened. Teaser copy on the envelope helps to increase the likelihood of that happening. So do hand-written addresses. A stamp (rather than a meter indicia) helps to increase the likelihood of the piece being opened, as does the stamp placed on the envelope slightly crooked. Now, a reality check. Although all this information is true, we are dealing on a much smaller scale. For companies such as Sears or Lillian Vernon whose mailing lists are in the millions, that small percentage makes a huge difference. We typically send out a mailing of a couple hundred pieces, perhaps a thousand. The small percentage difference in this example is so insignificant that we don't waste our time.

For years, people have said that if the envelope has a bulk stamp, people tend to toss it out. Based on Nancy's clutter seminars, people do not necessarily toss material with a bulk stamp. We first look and see if there is a bulk stamp, and if there is, then we look at the return address. If we don't know whom the envelope is from, then we tend to toss it out.

A couple of years ago, we did a test. We mailed an envelope from our office to the same test location. We found that if we used a postage meter rather than a stamp, the envelope was delivered two days sooner. If we used a typed address rather than a hand-written address, the envelope was delivered two days sooner. If we hand-write the address, use a stamp on the envelope, it get delivered—eventually!

Types of Postcards

There are thousands of different types of postcards. You could create a postcards that is your newsletter, a birthday card, a thank you card, an anniversary card, a Christmas card, a non-Christmas card, a 10 percent off card. Start to keep a file a samples of postcards (or mailing pieces) which you can design your own postcards. Here are a couple of suggestions.

The Veley Cartoon Update **Client Spotlight**

Bradford Veley, *Cartoonist and recovering clutterer*

In this edition of the Veley Cartoon Update, I'm delighted to introduce Nancy Miller, of ***Rounds, Miller & Associates****, a multi-service company specializing in business skills assistance. Those services include speaking, training, coaching, consulting and publishing.*

Nancy bought her first Veley cartoon 10 years ago and recently requested a custom-drawn illustration (below) to promote her services as a ***clutterologist****... Yes, you read that correctly -- Nancy helps disorganized people get out from under the clutter that causes chaos in their careers and lives. "Over the years," Nancy says, "we've used several of Brad's cartoons in our books and have been delighted with the reactions of people who've read them. We recently performed a postcard campaign focusing on our seminar attendees. The response has been great. People enjoy and keep the postcard -- when I go to their homes for a consultation, I can see the card -- they keep it."*

Nancy Miller, *Speaker, Trainer, Coach and Clutterologist Extraordinaire*

Rounds, Miller & Associates
6318 Ridgepath Court,
Rancho Palos Verdes, CA
90274-3248
Ph.: 310-544-9502
Nancy@RoundsMiller.com
www.RoundsMiller.com
www.Clutterology.com

Visit the website to order "Clutterology: Getting Rid of Clutter and Getting Organized" along with their other books and products.

Postcards are a terrific, cost-effective way to get your message out to a targeted audience, win new customers and stay in touch with existing ones! And when the postcard's artwork is memorable, touching or funny, you'll frequently find them displayed on various "walls of honor," including: refrigerators, office message boards, break-rooms, cubicles and the like. Think of it: the postcard you mailed for pennies has suddenly acquired the attention-getting power of a ***mini-billboard*** *(at no additional cost to you!) Sounds like a great deal to me.*

Thanks, Nancy! Here's to the next 10 years of doing business together!

And there's plenty of room on the other side for Nancy's return address, contact information, two logos, the addressee mailing label and this message:

"...You've taken the Clutterology seminar but still haven't gotten rid of the piles. Don't worry! Getting organized and reducing clutter is a learned skill. Nancy will come to your home or office to help you get started. Call to make an appointment or go to the website for more information."

VELEY

Cartoons, Humorous Illustrations, Freelance Writing & Editing by Bradford Veley
Ph.: 906-228-3229 www.bradveley.com E-mail: brad@bradveley.com Cartoon Mailing #249 Page 4 of 7

Testimonials

We could write a whole book on the importance of testimonials. Whenever possible, include what others have said about you. Use testimonials because they are more credible than just plain advertising copy. If you say the same thing, it sounds like bragging. Get a mix of testimonials: male/female, large/small companies, local city/state, and national/international.

What is that, you say? You do not have any testimonials? Never fear. Quote yourself. What is it that you are saying about your business, your service? Add the quote marks and people feel it's legitimate. For instance, we used a postcard quoting Mike.

> *"The Internet as it was designed, did, and still does,*
> *only one thing . . . send text."*
> *Mike Rounds*

Coupons

According to Elaine Floyd in her book Marketing With Newsletters, use these guidelines when designing coupons:

1. Place coupons to the outside edges of the page for easy removal (lower right-hand corner is best).

2. Track response by placing the coupon on the verso (back) page from the mailing label.

3. Include a graphic of the item offered for easy recognition.

4. Run a dashed-line border around the coupon.

5. Include an expiration date and any rules or exceptions.

6. Repeat your company name and, in small type, your address and phone number.

7. Place an icon of scissors near the top left-hand corner of the border.

8. Place the discount or offer in large type as the coupon's heading.

9. Make the coupon easy to remove by perforating around the edges (if your printing budget allows).

Parts of a Postcard

Although a postcard is small and simple, there are several distinctive parts to a postcard. When you put all of the parts of the postcard together, you can get a great, effective marketing piece.

Endorsements

Statistics from the Post Office state that 20 percent of a database will move each year. It's possible that in five years a database would be completely obsolete. Different databases have different characteristics. For instance, if you have a database of individuals over 60, they tend to move less frequently. College age individuals tend to move more frequently.

Endorsements represents a mailer's specific request for forwarding, return, or address correction (Return Service Requested, Address Service Requested, or Change Service Requested). By applying the proper endorsement, mail carriers knows exactly how to handle the mail should it be undeliverable as addressed.

We clean our list with every mailing (whether individual or bulk) by using the endorsement Return Service Requested. The Post Office will not forward this piece and will return the entire mail piece with the new address or reason for non-delivery when you use first-class postage. This is a free service provided by the Post Office. For bulk rate, each returned piece would cost an additional first-class postage rate.

The Post Office reads the mail with an OCR machine. Do not put your return address too far down or the Post Office will consider the return address as your delivery address.

The Post Office is your friend! They have several free items that are helpful in designing your postcard or your direct marketing piece. They are: Notice 67; D-1050251 Rev A, and the book Designing Letter and Reply Mail. Call your local Post Office Marketing Department for a copy.

Headline
Keep your headline to 11 words or fewer. Think about it this way: if you were driving down the highway at 55 miles per hour, could you read and understand the billboard you just passed? You have to grab people's attention; that's the job of the headline. An effective headline uses verbs.

The first ten words are more important than the next ten thousand! Some of these first ten words will be in the headline. They must be very carefully chosen so they will cause the client's eye to stop when it reaches your ad. You have only a second, more or less, to accomplish this feat, so your headline must have a basic emotional appeal. Use words which, even at a glance, penetrate the clients' subconscious and cause them to stop and consider. There are numerous words you can use in your headline to get the clients' attention.

Here are some examples. As you read these, notice how many grab your own interest and make you curious as to what the missing words in each partial headline might be:

Advice To ______ By
Discover/Discovery
Do Wonders With
Does Your
Don't Let
Free!
Giant
How I
How To
How You Can

Know About
Money Back
Name Your Mistakes That Cost
New
No More
Now You Can
Profits For You
Revealed
Save

Secrets
Take This Test
The Secret Of
Throw Away Your
We'll Help You
Who Else Wants
Where You Can
Why Did You
You Can
273 Ways To

When or where should headlines be used? In classified ads, in directories, in banner advertising, in e-zines, and in magazines just to name a few. In other words, almost everywhere.

Here are some award-winning headline ideas (according to the Journal of Advertising Research) to help you get your creative juices flowing:

Ask a question—offer an answer
- Are You Paying Too Many Taxes?
- Is Your Property Value Falling or Raising?

Arouse curiosity
- Ever Wonder How Your Cell Phone Finds You?
- Do You Know What Soda is Healthy for You?

Diametrically-opposed words
- How to Create Low-Cost High-Profit Products
- Simple Solutions to Complex Problems

Endorsement
- As Seen on TV
- As seen on Oprah
- 9 out of 10 dentist recommend

Facts or statistics
- 7 Habits of Highly Effective People
- The 10 Best Jobs in America
- 1,000 Places to See Before You Die

Familiar saying with a twist
- They Laughed When I Sat Down at the Piano, But When I Started to Play!
- They Laughed When I Started My Own Business
- They laughed when I ran that little $30 ad—but when I got 97 calls in only 3 days ...!
- They Laughed When I Decided To Teach My Children At Home

How to ...
- How to Win Friends and Influence People
- How to Read Literature Like a Professor : A Lively and Entertaining Guide to Reading Between the Lines
- How to Talk So Kids Will Listen & Listen So Kids Will Talk
- How To Cook Everything : Simple Recipes for Great Food

News or information
- Recent News Events Show That Security Systems Reduce Burglaries
- Celebrities Are Losing Weight Using The Latest Fad Diet! Should You?

Quotation
- "I'll resign before I allow the old procedures to be reinstated"
- "That's my life you're writing about so please get it correct"

Shocking or emotional statement
- Running Presents a Serious Health Risk
- Boy's Life Saved by His Pet Gerbil

Testimonial
- "We tried several methods for removing the grease from our carpets but nothing worked like FeeboT, the wonder cleaner"
- "We shopped over two dozen stores and couldn't find a better price than at Feebo's"

The most important part of the ad, a headline must stand out from the body copy. Keep the headline hard, fast, brief, and punchy. It should be in the largest font.

Sub-Head
Now that you caught the client's attention (just for a moment), add a sub-head to the headline. The best suggestion we have for sub-heads is to study book titles. The Self-Publishing Manual How to Write, Print and Sell Your Own Book by Dan Poynter or Clutterology® Getting Rid of Clutter and Getting Organized are titles with sub-titles.

The sub-head adds just a little more, or makes things a little clearer for the client. The font should be smaller than the headline font yet not as small as the body text.

Easy To Read
Design your ad or Web site so that it is easy to read. For instance, capitalize only the first letter of a word. ALL CAPS ARE 3X HARDER TO READ. IF YOU HAVE LESS THAN 11 WORDS IN YOUR HEADLINE, YOU COULD USE ALL CAPS. WE SUGGEST USING BOTH UPPER AND LOWER CASE.

If you remember your e-mail etiquette, sending a message in all upper case was like shouting. Designing an ad in all the same font is like shouting because the client cannot figure out what is important and what is not.

<u>Do not underline words in your copy, for two reasons</u>:

1. You will appear old-fashioned. Many of us learned to type on a typewriter. The only way to emphasis a word with a typewriter was to underline it. So, if you use underlining, you are dating yourself. What kind of impression do you want to make? What is the tone or slant, and would underlining compliment the tone?

2. An underlined word is associated with a hyperlink. Even if it is the printed word, people look at the underlined word and try to figure out the URL.

Use bold or italics instead of underlining. You can even change fonts (stay within a font family) or size of a font for emphasis.

Use restraint. You cannot put everything in an ad. You are excited about your service, so pick one, maybe two, key points. People don't have time to read or listen to even the good stuff because they have so much to do.

Be generous in your use of white space. What is white space, you say? White space is not filling up every inch with copy. Keep the font size a readable size (8+), and leave an appropriate margin on the top and bottom as well as the left and right side. Do not make your ad or Web site look like the small print of a contract! People know that the information is important (and usually legal) but it is just too hard to read the small print.

Use a serif font, not a sans serif font. A serif font has little tails and hands that, when reading a word, help to hook the letters together to form the word. Here is an example of sans serif and a serif font:

This is a sample of a sans serif font, typically an Arial font, which is good for headlines.

This is a sample of a serif font, typically a Times New Roman font. This type reads 12 percent faster than sans serif, which is good for text (stuff that needs to be read).

Don't Stop The Progress

Help the client to keep reading from one section (the headline) to the next section (the sub-head) to the next section (body copy). There are several ways to ensure that the client reads on.

Use an ellipse. You know these as the .... An ellipse is used when the quotation is intended to trail off and then pick up again on another part of the postcard or on the next page.

They all laughed ...

... when I sat down to play the piano.

If we were to say, "Knock knock," you would reply, "Who's there?" without any prompting. Using the ... the client wants to complete the sentence, complete the thought, or figure it out.

Decrease Line Spacing

The headline is the largest font. As the client reads down the ad, decrease the font size. This is a subtle way of telling the client what is most important, what is almost as important, what is important, and what is not so important.

Web Site

Your Web site is your four-color catalog. Its purpose is to make money for you—not to give your money to the Web site designer. Studies have shown that buyers who do not want or need to have the physical experience of the product prior to purchase are prime candidates for electronic catalog shopping.

The Web reduces the cost of creating and storing hundreds of pages of information to only pennies per day. You can direct your potential customers to your Web sites to view your electronic brochures in a fraction of the time, and from there to an electronic shopping cart to place orders.

There are a few key things to consider before you construct your site:

1. The Web is a gigantic library that customers can access for free—anytime they want to use it. Your Web site is like having a book in this library. Your home page is the cover of your book. This means that you can supply your advertising

materials, plus lots of other stuff for FREE. This is the only reason you need to justify having a Web site!

2. Your Web site is the electronic equivalent of a four-color catalog. Just because you can write and electronically print a lot of material at no additional charge doesn't mean you should. Your customers are time-constrained, and getting to the heart of what you have to say will assist them in getting and applying your information. Start to collect catalogs to generate ideas for your Web site. Is the front cover (home page) interesting? Is the order form (shopping cart) easy to understand? Are the items layout in an appearing way (interior pages)?

3. Your Web site is being created for the benefit of the customer, not for your own personal enjoyment or entertainment. Keep all the fancy graphics, animated cartoons, and other distracting elements off the site unless they are a critical part of the information.

Your Web site doesn't have to be fancy or exotic. It does have to be effective. Most Web site development software comes with templates that create a basic outline of the site for you. All you have to do is fill in the contents for the customer. You are not in a Web site or graphics design contest. The purpose of your Web site is to give customers the information they need to either make a decision or to educate themselves about you.

If the Web site is the equivalent to a catalog, here are some suggestions on how to layout and design your Web site catalog.

1. Think like a cataloger, not like a retailer. You are not selling face to face. Customers cannot ask questions, so anticipate their questions and supply the answers in the catalog. Use a *refer a friend* link.

2. Keep the order form simple. Include all the needed information. Ask for names of friends who would like to get the catalog.

3. Spell out the return policy, payment methods accepted, delivery times, sales tax, and shipping charges. Print the telephone number in large type on each page or spread.

4. Make sure the headlines are attention-grabbers that appeal to the customer's self-interest.

5. Put a date on the catalog to avoid confusion when another catalog is sent later.

6. Offer discounts for multiple orders. It works, and so do guarantees. They are often the deciding factor for uncertain catalog shoppers.

7. Include the address of the retail location, if there is one. Catalogs often drive retail sales.

8. Include sizing information if it's needed.

9. When fulfilling orders, include a related product sales piece to generate future sales.

10. Offer overnight delivery for an extra charge. People use catalogs for convenience.

Web Designers Myths
When you approach your Web designer, you may want to put all your trust in that person. Don't. As the business owner, your Web site must sell. Avoid they myths that your designers spouts.

H.I.T.S.
Since the birth of the Internet, the word *hits* is often used. If you were interviewing a Web site designer, they would extol their virtues and talk about how many hits a Web site gets because of their phenomenal colors, layout, graphics, spinning beer bottles, and so forth. With the dot.com explosion, for the first time in history labor told management how to run their companies.

Web site designers will often say that the greater the number of hits, the greater the exposure the Web site gets. Mike has a standard reply for that comment when organizations ask him to speak for them and are unable to pay for his full speaking fee. The conversation goes like this:

"Mike, we would like you to speak for the ABC organization but we are unable to pay for your full speaking fee. However, the ABC organization is such a great organization that we will give you a great deal of exposure!"

"Uhm, let me think about that. You are unable to pay for my speaking fee, so you want to expose me to more people that can't afford my services either. No, I think I'll pass."

When you hear the word *hits*, translate it into the acronym h.i.t.s. or How Idiots Track Success. Hits have little to do with the success of your business. They are a good starting point, just like the number of newspapers printed, audited subscribers of a magazine, and drive-by traffic for a storefront. If you cannot get people to take the next step (call, write, inquire, and stop in) you won't be in business long.

Here is a great example of a Web designer's great idea for getting hits gone bust.

If you were planning a trip to Washington DC and wanted to take a tour of the White House, most people would type in www.WhiteHouse.com without thinking. Dot com is the most common extension. However, the site that you should go to for tours of the White House is www.WhiteHouse.gov. The idea of using dot com was to capitalize on people not thinking.

The dot com site was an adult entertainment site. When kids discovered that WhiteHouse.com was an adult site, the information spread like wild fire. Every school and library had to block the dot com site to prevent kids from entering the site.

The important question to make this scheme work is what do people wanting a tour of the White House and a porn site have in common. Nothing. The site had tons of hits, and few sales. Since that time it has changed many times in the past couple of years.

BLOGS

You must have a BLOG (WE**B LOG**). For all practical purposes this is a big bulletin board that allows customers to leave any messages, pictures, videos, audios, or material they feel is related to the site's purpose.

Our definition of a BLOG is "dear diary, today I did . . ." The question that you need to ask regardless of what your Web designers says, "Will a BLOG bring me more business"?

Before you decide to BLOG, be sure that it is advantageous to you and to your business before you decide to create one. Apply Rule #1—ask yourself is that expenditure (of time and money) will make a difference between the customer ordering and not ordering?

Most BLOGs are usually opinions rather than facts. Donny Deutsch in one of his programs suggested that you get bloggers to talk about you—great a buzz about you!

For more information about blogs go to www.Bobology.com. Bob Cohen frequently teaches several classes at the community colleges.

Search Engines

You have to do this and that to get to the top of the search engines. Most people don't know how to use a search engine or how to find what they are looking for. Providing a massive list of meta-tags (index words) will help somewhat. The best way to get people to your Web site is to use conventional advertising to get your URL in their hands so they can go directly to your site.

Rule #2: Speed costs, so asking yourself how fast you want to go now applies to search engine listing and has given rise to a specialized service called Search Engine Listing and Optimization. If you want your site to be listed rapidly and to control the content and listing hierarchy, you will have to invest both time and money to get listed with the major engines.

The two possible exceptions are DMOZ http://dmoz.org and Google www.Google.com where you can still add your URL for free.

If search engine positioning is critical to your success, the best answer is to use a firm that specializes in search engine optimization such as Attach USA (www.AttachUSA.com). Search engine optimization firms have a staff of professionals who monitor and understand what is required for proper positioning and listing with the engines.

Mistakes To Avoid

Many times the Web site forgets the call to action. What do you want people to do? It's not that people are stupid it's that they don't have time to think what the next step is—so tell them.

Call To Action

For our small business, we cannot afford to wait around for a customer to someday buy from us. We need their money now, today, this week, this month, or this quarter.

Don't be shy, be bold! *Call*, *write*, *e-mail*, or *stop by* are all calls to actions. Can you make *your* call to action a little stronger? Use a deadline. Create a sense of urgency.

Other typical calls to action are:

1. Call our toll free number within the next hour and receive _____.

2. Offer expires _____.

3. Visit our Web site before ______ for a free bonus.

4. Visit our Web site to buy now.

5. Visit our Web site to learn more

6. Visit our Web site Save!!

7. Click here to _____.

8. Please Retweet Me!

Put an aura of timeliness to it: *Prices guaranteed through Midnight Saturday night. Offer expires June 31, 2015.* Make sure that people order **now**. What happens if they order July 1? Well, the 50 percent reduction is guaranteed only through the end of June so act now . . . .

When using the *visit our Web site*, be specific. It is not enough of an incentive for most people to just visit your Web site. Make the offer compelling.

Other great words to use are: call today, get involved, and shop now for the best selection.

Tell Them

People don't always know what your product is, how to use your product or what to do with your product. Most people don't have time to think. So, your job is to spoon feed the information to them until they say, "Eureka, that's just what I need!"

We love a Jack in the Box tray liner for Jack Cash Card. Instead of just saying, "Buy the card," they list 52 holidays when the card would make a great gift. Besides the standard holidays like Christmas, Halloween, and Easter are some less known (celebrated) holidays like Arbor Day, National Sibling Day, and National Nut Day.

When you have read all 52 holidays, you mind may say something like, "oh, hey, Dad's birthday is coming up." "I haven't seen Aunt Rita, I should get ..."

Below is another great example of a call to action. Rosemary is a charity and instead of saying, "We need you" they tell you specifically how you can help.

When you finish reading this, you may say to yourself, "Hey I have wrapping paper in my closet with a couple unused backpacks." Things you won't have thought of by yourself if they charity had just said, "send money!"

Below is another great example of a call to action. It is for a charity, and instead of saying, "We need you" they tell you specifically how you can help.

HELP MAKE IT HAPPEN . . .
BE A ROSEMARY STAR PLAYER!

Share Your Time

- Tutor a child
- Volunteer at special events in the office or organize a gift drive
- Become a foster parent or provide respite care for foster children
- During the holidays, volunteer as a gift wrapper; caroler or stocking stuffer

Share Your Experience

- Teach our children your special skill (cooking, painting, sports, etc.)
- Bring your professional skills to one of our committees
- Share your professional knowledge with our teens

Share Your Resources

- Make a personal donation, including: cash, gift certificates, book bags, arts/craft supplies, disposable cameras, party supplies
- Encourage your coworkers, company or organization to support our children through its matching gifts program
- Include Rosemary in your will and assure help stays available for the children of the future
- Designate Rosemary in your United Way pledge

Sweeten the Deal

Buy 2 get 50% off

Buy 1 for $19.99; 2nd for 1¢

Buy 1 get 1 FREE!

There is a 40 percent higher response rate to *buy 1 get 1 free* because of the word FREE!

If possible, add a free gift to your offer. In the English language, this is grammatically redundant because a gift is free. From an advertising point of view, three times as many people will respond to a *free gift* compared to a gift.

If you are providing a service, be sure to let your customer know what additional service you have given for free. Did you underestimate how long the project would take? On your invoice state:

5 hours of additional work .... No Charge (NC)

There is a book called *The Tipping Point* by Malcolm Gladwell; which documents why and how when using buy one get one free isn't more expensive than the other two.

According to the *Cheapskate Monthly*, December 2001 (www.CheapSkateMonthly.com), numerical signs such as "Two for the price of one or Limited three per person, cause shoppers to buy 30 to 90 percent more than they otherwise would. This happens even if the item isn't on sale." So to increase sales, you may want to limit the number of items with a specific offer.

During the 2009 Super Bowl, Denny's ran an ad for a free Grand Slam breakfast from 6 a.m. to 2 p.m. following the Super Bowl. Estimates were that they spent three million dollars on airtime (excluding production and talent costs), and gave away two million breakfasts at $5.99 each.

They received over 50 million dollars in news coverage and their Web site had so many hits that it was occasionally down. The best part (the way Denny's made money) of this is that most people would go to Denny's with a friend. We would guess that only 50 percent would order the Grand Slam breakfast (generating revenue). Also, this campaign got people back to Denny's.

Layout of Web Site

Obviously, since this is the electronic equivalent of a catalog, you can place anything on the Web site that makes sense for your marketing needs. Let's examine the specifics of what is available to you and why you might or might not want to include it in your site.

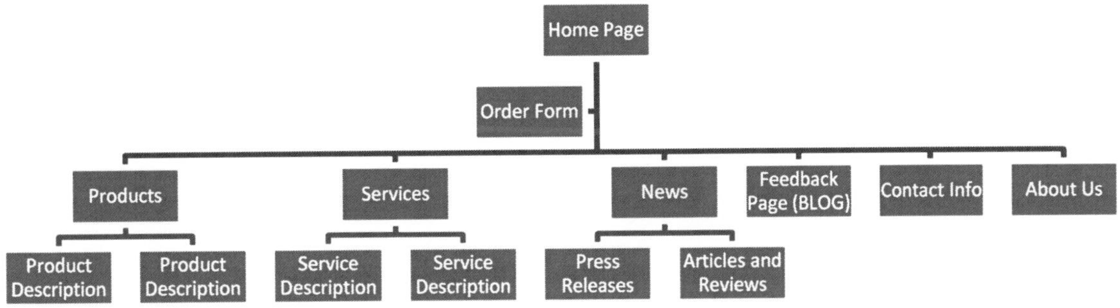

Home Page

Access to a Web site starts with the home page. It is called the home page to indicate its role as a starting point. Although it looks exactly the same as any Web page, its operation is radically different. The home page contains the URL (Universal Resource Locator) or address of the site plus hidden key or profile words search engines use to find your Web site.

From the home page, customers can access other sources of information by clicking on text or symbols that have been predesignated as a link point. The text that will link to other material (hypertext links) is different from other text in that it is usually shown in a different color and is underlined (for example www.RoundsMiller.com).

Think of the home page as the cover of your book, or the entry point into your catalog. Although you can make it as fanciful and animated as your imagination will allow, the time to download it onto a customer's computer, coupled with its appropriateness to the material contained within the site, becomes a prime consideration in the design.

Ideally, the home page should download in ten seconds or less when the customer is using a 28.8 kbps modem. Most of the better Web site authoring software programs contains download estimators that show what happens to the download time with the addition of each piece of text or graphics.

The home page should include:

Table of Contents
If your site is search enabled (which it should be if it has more than a few pages), make sure there is a search box on the home page. Since the customer cannot flip through the pages of a Web site like they can through a catalog, it becomes essential that you make it as easy as possible for them to find what they are looking for.

There are two effective approaches to this requirement:

1. An alphabetized and hyperlinked table of contents where customers can look up what they want and click on the link. This will automatically connect them to the item. An easy-to-use linked table of contents on the home page is a must to make sure the customer can find what he or she is looking for—fast. (Put it in the margins so the customer can get to it from anywhere inside the site!)

2. A site search engine allows customers the opportunity to type what they know into a box and let the engine find it for them. Some customers don't want to look things up alphabetically, or they may have a key word in a description of an item rather than its proper title.

Make the layout logical and simple to navigate. Customers are there to gather information, not to get lost exploring a labyrinth. If you think the customer may want or need more information, write short pages to begin with and then link them to longer copy as an option.

Page Title
The browser window should display your site's title and a brief description. Use language that will be informative in bookmark lists and search engines.

Logo and Tagline
Include your company name and/or logo in its expected location—the top left hand corner of the page. Use your logo on every page. It's the continuity the customer sees. It's your branding. Identify what your site is all about, preferably in a one-sentence tagline. Don't let anyone wonder what you do or what you sell. For a service company, this could be a variation on your elevator story.

Contact Information
Contact information must be easy to find. If possible, include it on every page of your site. This includes name, address, telephone, 800 or toll free telephone number, customer service hours, and e-mail.

Don't hide from your customers. Some people do need to contact you by phone or are curious about what city you are located in. It doesn't mean that they will show up at your door step. Many times, a Web site is judge if it is legitimate or just a scam when people check the contact information. The less information that's there, the more you are hiding. The more that you are hiding, the more distrusted you become.

Copyright Notice
It's often advantageous to post the copyright notice on the home page to advise customers that the site's contents are proprietary and not to be copied or used without your specific written permission. This issue can become critical if you are publishing tips, insights, articles, or other information that might be copied by customers and reprinted as their own.

External Links
If there are resources, either internally on your site or externally on others sites—such as maps, driving directions, or times and places of related events—you feel will be of interest to customers, make it easy for people to access them by creating hyperlinks.

Webmaster
If there is a problem with a site (suggestions, correction and broken links), customers will usually pass it along to the person designated as the site designer (Webmaster). This link automatically activates the Webmaster's e-mail.

Sign In and Sign Up
If your site requires users to log in for access, make the log in area prominent on the home page. If you plan to solicit user e-mail addresses for a newsletter or other communication, ask for the sign up on every page, including the home page.

Product and/or Service Page
This is what will interest most people with buying power (money). Since the Web site has almost unlimited capability (at virtually no cost) to create and display descriptions, specifications, applications, and other pertinent details of what you are offering, this is the perfect place to do it. There are a variety of ways to list and link these descriptions. The cleanest is to list each product or service and then link it to a page that contains short (less than 100 words), medium (between 100 and 250 words), and long (more than 500 words) descriptions about the item.

When you present the information in this manner, you give customers an active choice of how much (or how little) they need in order to get enough information to make a decision about the product or service.

Pictures (Low-Resolution)
If there is a reason why the Web's popularity exploded over the old text system, it has to be graphics and color. Digital photography has made it simple and inexpensive to provide full color images of goods. Services that demonstrate to the customer the appearance and functions of what you are offering can be either photos or video.

If you have bought or sold something on eBay, you know the importance of the picture. When the image is available, the product sells better than an auction without an image. People will look at the image and may not even read the description.

FAQ's Page
This page anticipates the **f**requently **a**sked **q**uestions a person might have about your products or services. It helps eliminate the phone calls or e-mails that become repetitive so you can concentrate on getting and handling more business.

PR or Media Page
When you do something new and different, it's a good idea to put out a press release. If you have ever had any experience with press releases, you know they are printed as editor's choice material because you don't pay for the space. The end result is that most releases do not get printed.

For selling your services, this is where background information, industry information, and commercial viability of information articles are placed.

Privacy Policy
If you collect any information from your users, have a clearly written and easily found Privacy Policy. Search the Internet for *sample privacy policy.* The BBB Online has a good examples for you to work from.

Reviews and Articles Page
Whenever you receive any kind of written review (especially if it is positive) you should immediately obtain reprint rights and post it on your Web site. These serve as testimonials. Since they are written by an independent party (such as a magazine or newspaper) they are perceived as being unbiased.

There are two types of articles, those written about you and those written by you. The articles written by you would include tips and ideas to help people.

Hidden Pages
There are a lot of things to which you want only selected people to have access and this is where we put them. (NOTE: These pages should NEVER have a link ANYWHERE on the site! The only way a customer should know they exist is because you have given them the URL.) These include notes and handouts, material developed for a specific group rather than for public, or a special offer that's only being made available to selected customers.

Another popular use of these pages is for material (an e-book) that is sold and can only be accessed by people who have been given the exact URL. Other items include maps with driving directions to home offices, price lists, customer interaction documents, and other proprietary information.

Mission Statement Page and About Us Page
Frequently people want to know your philosophy. Create a page for this information. Customers may want to know who you are and why they should trust you. An About Us page is the expected place to give this information.

Autoresponders
Autoresponders gratify customers by sending an e-mail message containing the information that the customer immediately and without additional labor.

You can get your own free autoresponders at www.GetResponse.com and program them to deliver materials to the respondent and, at the same time, capture their e-mail address. Once you have the respondent on a qualified e-mail list, you can create and deliver highly targeted material at virtually no cost.

These fully automated systems deliver information instantly to your prospects, and then can automatically follow up with personalized messages any number of times over the coming days, weeks, or months.

Social Networking and Social Media

You may want to consider these new forms for possible advertising. Even though they are popular, doesn't mean that they are a good place to advertise. Does your customer hang out here in the first place? If they are hanging out, are they also buying? Investigate before you spend lots of money or time trying to make it work.

Facebook, Twitter, LinkedIn and blogs are the top four social media tools used by marketers (in that order). Facebook has eclipsed Twitter in 2010. Is Social Networking good for your? Is Social Networking good for our business? It's hard to say. The rules are being made up as we go along.

Facebook (since 2004) is a free-access social networking. Users can join networks organized by city, workplace, school, and region to connect and interact with other people. People can also add friends and send them messages, and update their personal profiles to notify friends about themselves. Is having a Facebook **fan page** and getting a huge number of fans all that needs to be done? How do you convert fans into clients? Can it be done?

Here is my definition of Facebook—my hometown newspaper. It has the major business news (my business collogues who are self-promoting and telling me what they are doing). It has the hometown sports section where the team isn't winning and you looked at the pictures to see who's kid was playing and how good (and tall) the kid was. There are family and friends that tell you (and post pictures) about their kids, trips and social activities. And then there are the comics. The silly game that my brother is playing that I still can't figure out. He flings something at me and is buying something and I thing this stuff is a waste of time.

However, later in the day, I'm talking to Mike and mentioned, "oh, did you see that Hector is giving a presentation in Singapore and will be getting together with my brother next week." "How'd you know that?" I saw it on Facebook. And all I managed to do was skim the headlines. www.Facebook.com Mari Smith seems to have good content and free webinars about using Facebook as a business tool. www.MariSmith.com

LinkedIn (since 2003) is a business-oriented social networking site mainly used for professional networking. As of May 2009, it had more than 40 million registered users, spanning 170 industries. You may understand how LinkedIn works for you personally (kinda like a electronic resume) but does that work for your small business marketing? www.LinkedIn.com Lewis Howes seems to have good content about using LinkedIn as a business tool. www.LewisHowes.com

MySpace (since 2003) is a social networking Web site with an interactive, user-submitted network of friends, personal profiles, blogs, groups, photos, music, and videos for teenagers and adults internationally. MySpace became the most popular social networking site in the United States in June of 2006. MySpace had **layoffs** June 2009. The 100 millionth account was created on August 9, 2006, in the Netherlands. www.MySpace.com

StumbleUpon (since 2007) is an Internet community that allows its users to discover and rate Web pages, photos, and videos. It is a personalized recommendation engine which uses peer and social-networking principles. www.StumbleUpon.com

Twitter (since 2006) is a free social networking and micro-blogging service that enables its users to send and read each others' updates, known as tweets. Tweets are text-based posts of up to 140 characters, displayed on the author's profile page and delivered to other users-known as followers-who have subscribed to them. Senders can restrict delivery to those in their circle of friends or, by default, allow open access. Users can send and receive tweets via the Twitter Web site, Short Message Service (SMS) or external applications. The service is free over the Internet, but using SMS may incur phone service provider fees. How do you write tweets that will result in more interactions that will get retweeted? http://twitter.com

Other social networking Web sites are: www.Bebo.com; www.Classmates.com; www.Flickr.com; www.Orkut.com and www.Xanga.com. 360.yahoo.com closed in July 2009.

A couple of good (perhaps great sources are www.SocialMediaExaminer.com. They have tutorials that are wonderful. Sign up for their webinars as they are informative. Their subscription (which is daily) became overwhelming. I started to just read the headline and if it didn't interest me, I deleted it. Very effective.

HootSuite is another great resource. This is the only way that I can say up-to-date on my weekly tweets. I outline, organize and schedule them a quarter at a time. If I had to do them on a daily bases, I would fail this task. I don't even check Facebook daily.

Hiring A Web Designer

If you decide to hire someone to create your Web site, our suggestion is that you have someone create your **homepage**, a couple of **interior pages** and the **shopping cart**. Most people know how to use a keyboard so inputting and creating the other pages is just a matter of typing it in.

There are several different Web sites that provide Web designers.

Register and post your project: someone creates a homepage, a couple of interior pages and the shopping cart. If you are uncomfortable working with someone from a foreign country, you can exclude them. You will get replies from different freelancers and they will quote you their price. They have samples and a portfolio to view their work, a résumé and feedback from people that have used them. Go to www.Elance.com.

If you go to www.99designs.com you post a price. For instance: need a Web site created for $100. You will get a variety of replies ranging from just the home page to the complete Web site for that fixed price.

If you want a free Web site for your business (free means it will include advertising for the company that gives you the Web site) go to www.FreeWebs.com and follow their instructions for creating a free Web site.

The Web is a powerful business tool! Use it as a business tool to work with your business systems. Expect that the Web is the only thing necessary; you will be sorely disappointed and perhaps even end up broke.

What's In It For Them (WIIFT)?

You may have heard this before, Sell the sizzle, not the steak. That means sell the benefits, not the features. Is a coffee maker in a hotel room a feature or a benefit? For the longest time, although we understood the words, we did not understand the concept. Another way of saying it is, which means ...

For example, a house has 14 bathrooms (the feature) which means that you will never have to wait to use the bathroom (the benefit). Here is an exercise. On a piece of paper write down all the features of your product. Add which means and then list one benefit of the features.

Features		Benefits
2 bathrooms	which means	You and your spouse have separate bathrooms
Close to school	which means	When you plan to sell the house it will sell quickly to a family with kids
	which means	
	which means	

Now, write the ad with just the benefits. Sometimes you will have to say what the feature is. Sometimes you may want to use the transition phrase, which means, and sometimes you can use other transition phrases for variety. By using this method, you should be able to design a benefits-oriented ad.

Swipe File

This is a collection of things you liked or did not like. When it's time to sit down to design and layout an ad or flyer, you don't have to start with a blank piece of paper. Go to your swipe file (also called an idea file) and let those creative juices flow. You are not swiping anything; you're just using the samples as a starting place to create your own idea. Search for interesting tips, facts, and jokes to put in your swipe file.

Your Exercise

Use this worksheet to think out your ad and to be certain you didn't leave out anything important.

What is your purpose for sending out this postcard? Introduce your business/service/product to potential clients. Explain in detail:

____

____

Who should be receiving this postcard?

____

____

What type of action do you want the person to take when he or she gets your postcard?

____

____

What kind of impression do you want to make? What is the tone or slant of this card?

____

____

What can you offer the client as an incentive to try or sample? What is the enticement? When does this expire?

____

____

What is your message?

____

____

Include:

Name of company:	Business address:	Internet address:
Name of product/service:	Business phone:	Social network:
Primary contact name:	Business hours:	

Products

What do information products have to do with marketing your services? Plenty, because they serve the multiple purpose of positioning you as an expert in your field, provide credible marketing materials, and serve as a revenue generation system that can double or triple your income!

Products serve the multiple purpose of positioning you as an expert in your field, provide the most credible marketing materials you can create, and serve as a revenue generation system that can multiply your organizing income!

There have always been credibility reasons for professionals to create information and support products and sending your book or other material to a potential client positions you as a published expert and provides greater credibility on the topic than a person who doesn't have published materials.

The other concern is that Professional Organizers are service providers and when we're not providing services, we're not making money. The answer to this dilemma is to provide information products that generate revenues when we're not on the platform and even while we're sleeping.

Books are the classic technique and in today's rapidly changing world, there are a variety of economical, profitable methods available that will enhance and increase your revenue stream.

This is going to be a quick overview of some of the products you can create. If you're serious about this area, check out Self-Publishing for the Clueless 189144036-1 available from www.RoundsMiller.com. For $25, you'll get an hour of audio and a 100+ page manual that'll show you, in detail, everything you need to know.

Books

Of all the information delivery vehicles you can create, a book still gives the most credibility and opens the most doors for profits.

Workbooks or how to books are among the best selling types of books in the world and will probably get you the maximum return on your investment of time.

My partner and I have authored several books. They, like this manual, are how to books, workbooks, manuals, or guidebooks—whichever term you prefer.

We create them because they position us as experts and authorities in the topics we have selected to address plus when we offer our programs at college seminars and workshops, they provide us with a revenue-generating tool.

Mini-Books

Based on results, the best credibility enhancer is a book. If you want to create a more definitive focus or expand your area of expertise, I'll highly recommend doing a series of tips mini-books to demonstrate your expertise on a related topic without having to write and publish an entire new book.

If you want to produce full color, sixteen page, mini-books for as little as 15¢ each in a quantity of one on your ink jet printer, you can use the book fold option in Microsoft Word.

Our book E-Publishing for the Clueless available from www.RoundsMiller.com has complete details, illustrations, and pre-configured templates for both the interior and the cover.

Audio

Second to books, audio is the best information product you can generate because it's a non-intrusive medium. If you think about it, even though books are highly revered and respected, they require that the reader dedicate time to read. Video material requires that you dedicate time, and unique equipment. Audio can be multi-tasked while working, driving, or jogging.

What you record on audio is pretty much up to you. The best audio material doesn't need a visual component. That means that if the audio has to be accompanied by pictures, a workbook, or effort other than listening, it's not quite as effective as something that stands alone naturally.

The most common audio products are live recordings. Digital recorders are under $100 and small enough to fit into your pocket or clip on your belt. With a digital master, you can create any other medium you want including CD's.

On the other hand, organizational training programs usually have a high visual content, so the use of video helps to reinforce that concept especially, if you're using graphs, charts, props, or other visual aids.

Another technique requires a little more equipment and an interviewer. It's fun and highly saleable. Its basic format is an interview style and it's different because you write down 100+ questions about your topic. This style is good if your audience follows you to the rest room to ask you questions after the program is over or if you are a trainer and have more material than the program allows time for.

When it's done, you'll have 101 of the most commonly asked questions about the topic as answered by you, one of the country's leading authorities.

If you're going to record, consider getting an inexpensive recording and editing software package. You can get free Windows audio recording and editing software from Audacity (http://audacity.sourceforge.net) that will let record, edit, mix, add sound effects and convert it to just about any audio format, CD or MP3, that's currently popular. It allows you to stick a microphone into your computer and record it directly. Since it's an editor, you'll be recording, editing, and processing perfect digital masters every time.

Another technique that seems to sell well is taking your recorded material, dividing it into 12-18 modules, and recording it as a training set. Look at Tony Robbins or Stephen Covey—that's what they've done. Current statistics say that the average commuter spends about 20 minutes on a commute, so 20 minute audio products are the most expeditious length.

Breaking up material into short sound bites, whether it's practicing telephone techniques or psyching yourself up to be a better person, will keep the listeners' attention longer. The media has proven that sound bites work best so if you were doing this kind of project, stay with the short concepts and make the product conform to what the public says it wants.

You can get any kind of AV packaging you need, including blank media labels, and duplication equipment, at inexpensive prices from Shop4Tech, 4664 Mission Blvd, Montclair, CA 91763, 1-866-907-3626, www.Shop4Tech.com.

E-Books

The latest delivery vehicle is to use the internet (or CD-ROM) to offer the reader a lot of information in a very efficient manner.

There are several schools of thought about the delivery of e-books that are determined by how much time you personally want to spend fulfilling the orders.

On one end of the spectrum, there are fully automated shopping cart delivery systems that allow the client to order the book, pay for it with a credit card, download and read and/or print it out.

The systems verifies the client's credit card, deposits the money in your bank account, and delivers the material without you having to do anything other than spend the money and pay your taxes.

The more exotic systems allow you to decide how many copies of the e-book the client can download, whether it can be printed out or simply read on the screen, or whether the entire file can be downloaded and shared with others.

Our book E-Publishing for the Clueless available from www.RoundsMiller.com has complete details and all of the software necessary to be e-published for free. It includes books, audio podcasts, video podcasts, BLOGS, and all the resources you'll need.

Newsletters

This is one of those areas where two people will give you four opinions as to whether or not it's profitable to write newsletters. Projects like newsletters take time and as a service provider, that's what you're selling. Make sure that there's a positive return on investment before you embark on one of these ventures.

Here's our opinion about newsletters based on observations and cash flow.

1. Newsletters are a good idea if:

    - You can get people to pay for a newsletter.
    - You're writing and distributing newsletters to keep your name and services in front of clients and/or prospects who can actually hire you.
    - You're using your newsletter as a forced method of compiling information that you plan to publish in the near future.
    - You can get sponsors to pay you (either cash or trade) to write and distribute your newsletter.
    - Your newsletter is getting you orders for your products or services.

2. Newsletters are not a good idea if:

    - You're writing them because your ego says you should.
    - You're not getting any business or referrals from them.
    - You're not making enough money to pay for the newsletter's hard costs plus your time.
    - Somebody else who doesn't have to do the work said you should do it.

Notice that we did NOT discriminate or differentiate between paper or electronic newsletters. The uninformed will tell you that an e-newsletter is OK because it's virtually free to distribute compared to the printing, handling, and postage costs of a paper version.

The reality is that the publication has to show a profit or it's not worth writing and distributing it, regardless of the delivery method. Even if you breakeven on the hard costs, you're still throwing away your time and as we've already noted, it's the most valuable commodity you've got.

Tom Antion's e-mail newsletter (www.Antion.com) is a great example of the right way to do it. He uses it to sell lots of products, advertise his world famous Butt Camp, and get loads of people to sign up for his tele-seminars. His return on investment is outstanding and his reputation as an expert in this field is growing with each issue.

Here's a special noteworthy consideration: if your industry is overcrowded with printed newsletters, consider producing an audio newsletter. Current costs are less than $1 per CD, recorded, reproduced, and mailed, and these will surely get listened to, and perhaps passed on.

The formats can vary from articles read for audio to a one-on-one interview with current industry leaders. If you're uncomfortable with this concept, professional duplicating businesses have lists of narrators who will record the materials for you.

Articles

Here's another area of questionable return unless it's done properly. Writing articles is time consuming and seeing your name in print is a poor return on investment unless you're getting cash business in return.

We've written monthly columns for fee and free, and both have had mixed results. Editors, especially trade journal editors and those who publish industry specific newsletters, are in need of experts to write good, meaty articles that will enhance the credibility of their publication.

As a general rule, they don't care about your investment of time and will appeal to your ego saying that "your efforts will enhance your credibility" because you're now published.

Re-read the pros and cons of newsletters on the previous page as they are equally appropriate here when writing articles.

Ed Rigsbee (www.Rigsbee.com) taught us how to make writing articles pay off. He's made his fame and fortune with his partnering techniques and freely shares the techniques with others. Here's his secret to success with articles:

- Write articles for trade journals that represent the industry or discipline where you are likely to get hired.

- After you've written articles for a specific target industry, could you generalize the article and put them on your Web site with permission to reprint them as long as you get the credit.

Permission to reprint articles by _____ at no charge is granted with the agreement that the article bio be included following each article used and one copy of the publication in which the article is published be provided to _____. A fee of $300 per article will be expected for articles published without the closing bio and contact information.

- Notify anybody you think will be a good source of notoriety that the articles are available for reprint for FREE.
- Don't jump at the chance to write articles for somebody unless you can justify the investment in time.

The more exposure you gain through an organization's printed material, the more familiar you become. When it's time to hire an organizer, your name, your expertise, and perhaps your face will be a common element in their business experience.

DVDs

The way to go is DVD since all the new computers contain digital video editing software and over 75 percent of them will play (and record) DVDs.

If you want to be your own video producer, director, and distributor, hand-held video camera systems that shoot directly to a flash memory drive are less than $100 and you can get a complete, high-definition camera and sound system that records directly to hard drive for less than $1,000.

You can get a CD-ROM burner for about $30, a DVD burner for $99, and software packages to convert and copy to the DVD format for $20.

The Studio digital editing software is available for around $99 from Pinnacle Systems (www.PinnacleSys.com) that allows you to digitize, edit and create a variety of digital mediums including CD-ROMs and DVDs.

Microsoft has the Windows Media Recorder for FREE at www.Microsoft.com. This amazing piece of software allows you to take your video files and convert them for play on everything from a 28.8 modem on a Web site though direct play from a CD.

- Another is the material that you won't have time to cover in the training session. Consider recording the extra hours of material that are needed but that the organization just can't spare the time to have you deliver in person.
- If the training requires ongoing or updated sessions, consider using video to stay in touch or to conduct training without having to jump on an airplane and show up in person.
- This one sounds strange and you might be surprised at how well it works. Gather 10-20 questions from the attendees, answer them on video, and send the client the DVD together with permission to make as many copies as necessary. This is the next best thing to answering their questions from the platform plus it gives the added benefit of conducting a one-on-one session with the client.

Organizational Involvement

Of all the methods there are for promoting organizing services, nothing has ever proved to be more advantageous than joining an organization and getting involved.

Because Professional Organizers are hired for performance as opposed to presence, people with the power and authority to hire us need to be made aware of our skills, expertise, knowledge, and level of commitment to projects under our control.

Virtually all industries have numerous organizations (or associations) that can be advantageous to join. The key to success in this arena, however, is to not only join but to get involved with the organization.

People are curious about how others make their living, and no doubt you will have the opportunity to discuss your business and gain referrals. As society becomes more complex, membership in organizations becomes a way of meeting people with similar values and interests. The assumption is that prospects like to do business with people they know and trust.

The National Trade and Professional Associations Directory from Columbia Books (www.ColumbiaBooks.com) list 7,500 national trade associations, professional societies and labor unions. Five convenient indices enable you to look up associations by subject, budget, geographic area, acronym and executive director. Other features include: contact information, serial publications, upcoming convention schedule, membership and staff size, budget figures, and background information.

Historically, there's no better way to get business than by networking with people and organizations that are in either a position to hire you or to refer you simply because they know you and have first-hand experience of your capabilities. The halls of business success are lined with stories about how networking, contacts, and connections have played a significant role in the success of business people everywhere.

There are other auction sites that are popping up. We're familiar with www.cmarket.com/auction/BiddingForGood.action which is an auction site for charities. You may want to drop into this site and check out how they do things and what you would change.

This site has become a valuable resource for us. Here are some of the ways that we us it:

- With the current condition of the economy, you may be seeing a lot of empty advertising spaces including billboard and bus benches. Although the prices may be down, check out BiddingForGood and search the auctions to find if there are good deals for discounted advertising. We have found billboards, bus benches, a full page in USA Today (regional edition), full-page ads in an association publication.

- Search for words like billboard, advertising, full-page and full page. You may get the front cover, back cover, or some good deals for a fraction of the cost.

- If you are looking to attract customers, perhaps donating your product or service to an auction (or several) may draw the client's you're looking for.

- Look at the ad copy of the items. Would you be willing to spend your money on that item? If not, why not. Look over the site to get some good ideas what you would do on your Web site and what you won't do on your Web site. Are the key questions answered about what the product is?

- We have purchased several items that have been on our Bucket List (a life-long dream list). Nancy purchased a submarine ride for Mike.

You are unique. Bring those special qualities to the profession as a Professional Organizer. You will not be able to help everyone that comes to you. Build your network of colleagues and resources. And go out there and be successful. Let's organized the world!

Index

About the Author

Growing up, Nancy Miller was surrounded by garbage. Trash put food on the table. Her family owned the garbage service in Hutchinson, Minnesota, a small town that managed to create more refuse than one might imagine. No one knows clutter better than Nancy.

Like most Midwestern dreamers, she hopped a bus to Los Angeles, where she would work her way to the top. Now, all grown up, Nancy is an internationally-recognized expert on making space, helping people carve out the room they need to move, live, and create.

Over the past fifteen years, Nancy has achieved rock-star status in Personal Organizing circles. She sings her siren songs of simplicity and messages of minimalism to packed audiences (seated alphabetically in neat little rows) in over 150 performances each year. In 1997, Nancy was awarded the golden statue stars like her crave when she accepted "International Who's Who of Entrepreneurs" honors. (Following her own rule, when she brought the trophy home, she found something else to throw away or donate.)

She has earned numerous other awards, including the Golden Microphone Award for Speaking Excellence, awarded by the Greater Los Angeles Chapter of the National Speakers Association. She is also a past member of the National Association of Professional Organizers' Golden Circle. This elite designation recognizes Nancy's service in the War on Clutter and gives her a back-stage pass to professional development activities that will help her hone her craft, to secure her place in history as a decluttering legend.

Heralded as a modern-day Mary Poppins, Nancy wrote the books on getting organized, *Clutterology™ Getting Rid of Clutter and Getting Organized* and *The Clutter Bug Attacks Junk Mail, Spam and Telemarketers®*. During on-site consultations, Nancy collaborates with individuals, families, and businesses to ensure they have everything they need and want. And nothing they don't.

Neat woman. Neat ideas. Neat message.

If you are interested in additional books, CDs and videotapes, our Web site lists additional resources. For information on a consultation or speaking engagement with your group, please contact:

Nancy Miller, Clutterologist
6318 Ridgepath Court
Rancho Palos Verdes CA 90275-3248
310-544-9502
Nancy@Clutterology.com
www.Clutterology.com
http://clutterology.wordpress.com
http://www.facebook.com/pages/Clutterology/363987771780?v=wall
http://www.linkedin.com/in/clutterology
http://twitter.com/Clutterology